FIRE AND
FLAMES

FIRE AND FLAMES

a history of the german autonomist movement

written by Geronimo
introduction by George Katsiaficas
translation and afterword
by Gabriel Kuhn

FIRE AND FLAMES:
A History of the German Autonomist Movement
c. 2012 the respective contributors.

This edition
c. 2012 PM Press

Originally published in Germany as:
Geronimo. Feuer und Flamme. Zur Geschichte der Autonomen.
Berlin/Amsterdam: Edition ID-Archiv, 1990. This translation is based
on the fourth and final, slightly revised edition of 1995.

ISBN: 978-1-60486-097-9
LCCN: 2010916482

Cover and interior design by Josh MacPhee/Justseeds.org
Images provided by HKS 13 (http://plakat.nadir.org)
and other German archives.

PM Press
PO Box 23912
Oakland, CA 94623
www.pmpress.org

10 9 8 7 6 5 4 3 2 1

Printed in the USA on recycled paper by the Employee Owners of
Thomson-Shore in Dexter, MI.
www.thomsonshore.com

CONTENTS

INTRODUCTION
BY GEORGE KATSIAFICAS

MORE THAN A DECADE BEFORE THE SEATTLE protests against the WTO, tens of thousands of people in Berlin confronted a global gathering of the International Monetary Fund and the World Bank—the most powerful wizards of high finance, and they compelled the world's bankers to adjourn hastily a day earlier than planned. Between 1981 and 1984, hundreds of thousands of Germans marched for peace, and they helped bring an end to the nuclear arms race and the Cold War between the United States and USSR. Among the participants in these and many other actions were radical youth who had occupied hundreds of abandoned buildings and challenged patriarchy while also fighting against forms of domination in everyday life. Allied with farmers and ecologists, they successfully stopped the attempt of Germany's nuclear power industry to produce weapons-grade uranium. Out of the crucible of all these struggles, the autonomous movement, or Autonomen, was galvanized as a force resisting the corporate system *as a whole* and seeking a thoroughgoing revolution of it.

Autonomous social movements do not subscribe to one ideology—within their ranks, Marxist-Leninists fight the system alongside anarchist feminists and anti-imperialist Turks. They do not seek to capture nation-states but to destroy them. They want to abolish politics as we know it—as the playground for generals, politicians, and businessmen. They want to destroy the existing system because they see it as the cause of war, starvation, poverty, and daily monotony.

Autonome do not have one central organization. As one group acts, another is inspired to rise up, and they, in turn, galvanize yet others in a chain reaction of insurgency I understand as the "eros effect," as the emergence of massive social movements capable of transforming civil society. Autonome appear as the "black bloc" at demonstrations, and they gather in regional assemblies, but they have no fixed organizations or enduring spokespersons. In the past three decades, they have manifested themselves within peace movements and anti-nuclear movements. Today they help animate the global justice (or anti-corporate globalization) movement. From below, millions of people around the world have formulated a focus for international mobilizations: confront elite meetings of the institutions of the world economic system—a practical target whose universal meaning is profound. As stated above, no central organization dictated this focus. Rather millions of people autonomously developed it through their own thoughts and actions. Similarly, without central organization, some thirty million people around the world took to the streets on February 15, 2003, to protest the second U.S. war on Iraq, even before it had started.

As this global movement becomes increasingly aware of its own power, its strategy and impact is certain to become more focused. By creatively synthesizing direct-democratic forms of decision-making and militant popular resistance, social movements' grammar of autonomy and the eros effect embodies what I call "conscious spontaneity." Key tactical issues facing the global justice movement are contained in microcosmic form in the development of the European Autonomen.

Seldom mentioned—and almost never in complimentary terms—German radicals at the end of the twentieth century made significant contributions to world peace and justice. At a time when most people in the world's wealthy nations were immersed in a gluttonous reverie of consumerism, many German youth mobilized against that current. For more than a decade, a squatters' movement challenged governments for control of city centers. The German movement's resilience, its ability to find new adherents from generation to generation, is nothing short of remarkable. In the United States, after the high point of 1970, the movement largely failed to regenerate itself except in single-issue activism, sectarian groups of one dogmatic belief system or another, or individualized projects. In the 1980s and early 1990s, when Mumia Abu-Jamal and other long-term political prisoners had almost no support in the United States, German Autonomen publicized their cases and brought international attention to bear on American racism.

The Autonomen's fight against racism is one of their most impressive dimensions. Nowhere else in the political universe of Germany did people actually *do* anything to stop the anti-immigrant pogroms in the 1990s that broke out in formerly communist parts of the country after unification. In places like Hoyerswerda and Rostock, racist mobs attacked Vietnamese, Mozambicans, and Angolans. When the police and the public turned a blind eye, the autonomous movement mobilized to break the sieges by German racists. Once the police finally did react, it was to arrest antiracist street-fighters, not the neo-Nazi attackers, as might be assumed.

Despite economic modernization, Germans have yet to extricate themselves from their own variety of national pride and ethnocentrism. There is certainly widespread public repudiation and private abhorrence of Adolf Hitler's ill-begotten quests for world domination and racial purity, but beneath the surface, a powerful nationalist identity remains intact. We forget that while Hitler failed to build a lasting Third Reich, his extermination campaigns greatly affected the character and composition of surviving Germans. Today, dreams of German imperial prowess are greatly diminished, possibly even forever extinguished, but neo-Nazis, with their goal of keeping the imagined Aryan bloodline intact, remain a force with which to be reckoned.

One of the glaring weaknesses of Germans' identity is a preoccupation with their own nation. While some people regard themselves as human beings first and as members of a nation somewhere later, many Germans fetishize their own national characteristics, remaining locked within the prison-house of German nationality, if not consciously, then at least in assumptions made and possibilities excluded. Apparently, it is far easier to inherit through inertia the weight of the past than to overcome long-held identities—even for the best of those among us who wish to help humanity leap ahead of our present predicaments.

As the twentieth century ended, many Germans were relieved to read continuing press accounts of the demise of the Autonomen and hoped the movement had finally succumbed to the untiring corporate onslaught. Berlin was in the midst of its post–Cold War building boom and old Autonome neighborhoods were becoming increasingly gentrified. Although something of a legend in American activist circles, the German autonomous movement had never grown beyond the marginality it embraced as proof of its righteousness, and it finally seemed on the verge of extinction.

At the same time, the Green Party spawned by various grassroots movements had become part of the national government. With the connivance of a Green foreign minister, Joschka Fischer—a former radical street-fighter and *Sponti*—German troops were stationed outside the country for the first time since Hitler, and Germany enjoyed the long-denied status that any "normal" European power takes for granted. While abstaining from the Anglo-American attack on Iraq, Germany played an active role in the war on the Taliban and cooperated with the world's great powers in the Balkans. For whatever progress Germany has made in qualitatively transforming itself from a militaristic imperialist power into a nation supporting peace and justice, we must certainly thank the Autonomen.

European autonomous movements have inspired Americans—and not just in the United States. The influence of the Autonomen is evident in a variety of forms—the black blocs that have emerged on this side of the Atlantic being perhaps the most obvious. For years, many people inquired why there was only a single English-language volume about autonomous movements (my own book, *The Subversion of Politics*). Now, two decades after it first appeared, Geronimo's *Fire and Flames*, the first German text from within the ranks of the Autonomen to systematically examine the movement's historical trajectory, has been brought out in English. This translation coincides with a revival of interest in the Autonomen brought on by their "rebirth," after years of near invisibility, in the anti-G8 protests in and around Rostock in 2007. Apparently, although the fires of autonomous resistance had died down somewhat, its embers were quickly fanned back into a conflagration that continues to burn beneath the facade of people's acceptance of world leaders' neoliberal agenda.

As I reread it, *Fire and Flames* reminds me how when young Germans embarked upon their march against institutional power, they suffered terrible repression both from the entrenched forces of the state as well as from their former colleagues (like the Greens) who engaged in the "long march through the institutions." Despite the apparent co-optation of the Greens through their incorporation into the liberal wing of the political establishment, the German public is still quite far from embracing the autonomous movement. A new Left Party has emerged among reformed former communists of East Germany and militant trade unionists sick of the Social Democrats' long-standing betrayal of their own fundamental precepts. Neither of these constituencies, however, has any high regard for the Autonomen's antiauthoritarianism. I

"SOLIDARITY IS A WEAPON — STOP THE EXPLOITERS!"

would love to be proven wrong here, but there seems to be no break-through looming in the near future for the Autonomen—nothing like their expanded space for action and the wave of new squats after the fall of the Berlin Wall in 1989.

Written by a long-time activist, *Fire and Flames* comprehensively uncovers German movement dynamics from the 1960s to the 1990s. Here one can learn about the German extraparliamentary opposition (APO), the Frankfurt Spontis (spontaneitists), the communist sects, the antinuclear power movement, the squatters' movement, the movement against the expansion of the Frankfurt airport, the now-mythologized Hafenstraße in Hamburg, the antiglobalization, antiwar, and antifascist movements, the armed struggle and more. There is even a chapter on Autonomia in Italy.

Largely (and somewhat conspicuously) missing from these pages, however, are the autonomous struggles of women and the feminist critique of patriarchy. I would not conclude from his omission of femi-nism (the word does not appear once in the text) that Geronimo is therefore simply a sexist. I know him intimately—we have traveled to-gether, lived together, loved, laughed, and, as friends at close quarters sometimes do, quarreled. I can vouch that he has examined his own everyday life in relation to gender questions; he neither deems himself superior to women nor disregards them as comrades.

His nonfeminist position is rather based on a thought-out politi-cal evaluation of the meaning of the autonomous movement's uni-versality and the need for its unity—which he feels is threatened by what he regards as feminism's partiality. Rather than comprehending the universal in the specificity of feminism (or Black culture, or gay culture), that is, that we all benefit from the struggle to extinguish pa-triarchy, he locates the universal simply as it appears in a unified move-ment. In the first edition of his book, he included a few paragraphs on the topic of the autonomous women's movement. Honestly written, he could only conclude: "And so I have to laugh at my own inability and the knowledge that I'll never understand everything and just try to live with that."

Another lacuna that enervates the book's resonance is a failure to contextualize extensively the movement's international character. The Autonomen grew out of upsurges in Holland, Switzerland, and Italy; in turn, German activists have helped to foment similar move-ments in many lands—among them, Denmark, France, Spain, the Czech Republic, Sweden, and Mexico. The movement's international character is one of its most significant dimensions, yet the reader will not encounter that facet of its existence in this book's pages, with the sole exception of Italy.

I offer these criticisms of *Fire and Flames* in the spirit of friendship and solidarity. It is a book I heartily recommend and hope activists will more than read—it merits study and discussion, emulation, and critical transcendence.

Gwangju, South Korea, March 2008

TRANSLATOR'S NOTE AND GLOSSARY

GABRIEL KUHN

THE TRANSLATION OF *FEUER UND FLAMME* in this book is based on the fourth and final edition, published in 1995 by Edition ID-Archiv. Some paragraphs recollecting details of autonomous campaigns of the 1980s that seem of little relevance for the general history of the autonomous movement have been omitted. All omissions have been approved by the author. Where short explanations of names or events seemed necessary for non-German readers, they were added in square brackets.

Perhaps reflecting antiacademic tendencies among the Autonomen, the German original includes only very vague bibliographical references—a pattern the translation inevitably had to follow.

To this day, there is no standard English translation for the German term *autonom* in the context of the German *autonome Bewegung* (movement). Both "autonomous" and "autonomist" have been used, often interchangeably. There are three main reasons why "autonomous" is used consistently throughout this book:

1. In German, the term *autonomistisch*, which is the closest equivalent to "autonomist," has never been used in relation to the *autonome Bewegung*.

2. While "autonomism" implies a certain ideological orientation, one of the characteristics of the *autonome Bewegung* has always been its rejection of ideological definition.

3. Although the Italian *Autonomia* movement clearly influenced the *autonome Bewegung*, it was, in many ways, a very different phenomenon and spawned a tradition of libertarian Marxist thought that has little in common with the German Autonomen. It therefore appears useful to make a distinction in English between an Italian *autonomist* movement (and the school of libertarian Marxist thought that derived from it) and a German *autonomous* movement.

The following glossary includes a number of terms and, especially, acronyms that are used frequently in the book and that might require an explanation for non-German readers.

AL: Alternative Liste für Demokratie und Umweltschutz, or Alternative List for Democracy and Environmentalism. Founded in West Berlin in 1978, the AL basically served as West Berlin's Green Party chapter in the 1980s.

APO: Außerparlamentarische Opposition, or Extraparliamentary Opposition.

BI: Bürgerinitiative; literally, "citizens' initiatives," *Bürgerinitiativen* are grassroots initiatives whose politics can reach from conservative to radical; they emerged in the 1970s and remain a factor in German popular politics to this day.

CDU: Christlich-Demokratische Union Deutschlands, or Christian Democratic Union of Germany. Germany's main conservative party.

CSU: Christlich-Soziale Union in Bayern, or Christian Social Union of Bavaria. The CDU's Bavarian "sister party."

DGB: Deutscher Gewerkschaftsbund, or Confederation of German Trade Unions.

DKP: Deutsche Kommunistische Partei, or German Communist Party. Founded in 1968, the DKP claims to be the legitimate successor of the Kommunistische Partei Deutschlands (KPD), the original Communist Party of Germany, which was banned in West Germany in 1956.

FDP: Freie Demokratische Partei, or Free Democratic Party. Germany's main liberal party.

Greens/Green Party: "Greens" originally served as an umbrella term for activists of various environmentalist and direct-democratic grassroots initiatives that formed in the 1970s. Soon after the foundation of the Green Party (Die Grünen) in 1980 and the related institutionalization of the Green Movement, the term became almost exclusively used for Green Party members.

Jusos: Jungsozialistinnen und Jungsozialisten in der SPD, or Young Socialists in the SPD. Youth organization of the Social Democratic Party.

K-groups: "K" as in *kommunistisch*; various Marxist-Leninist parties and cadres founded in the wake of the 1960s student revolt.

KB: Kommunistischer Bund, or Communist Union, 1971–91. See "K-groups."

KBW: Kommunistischer Bund Westdeutschland, or Communist Union of West Germany, 1973–85. See "K-groups."

KPD: Kommunistische Partei Deutschlands, or Communist Party of Germany. Founded in 1919, the KPD was banned in West Germany in 1956. In East Germany, the KPD merged with the SPD in 1946 to form the Sozialistische Einheitspartei Deutschlands (SED), or Socialist Unity Party of Germany, which governed East Germany.

KPD-AO: Kommunistische Partei Deutschlands–Aufbauorganisation, or Communist Party of Germany–Pre-party Organization, 1970–80 (from 1971 officially only KPD). See "K-groups."

KPD-ML: Kommunistische Partei Deutschlands–Marxisten-Leninisten, or Communist Party of Germany–Marxists-Leninists, 1968–86. See "K-groups."

RAF: Rote Armee Fraktion, or Red Army Faction, urban guerrilla group founded in 1970.

RZ: Revolutionäre Zellen, or Revolutionary Cells, a network of independent left-wing groups engaged in militant direct action, founded in the 1970s; Rote Zora was a related network of women activists.

Second (2ⁿᵈ) of June Movement: Bewegung 2. Juni, urban guerrilla group founded in 1972.

SEK: Spezialeinsatzkommando, SWAT teams of the German police.

SDS: Sozialistischer Deutscher Studentenbund, or Socialist German Student Union. The main radical student organization in the 1960s student revolt.

SPD: Sozialdemokratische Partei Deutschlands, or Social Democratic Party of Germany.

Spontis: derived from *spontan* (spontaneous), Spontis were political activists rejecting formal organization and focusing on creative interventions in everyday life, with strong cultural, artistic, and also humorous elements.

West Germany and **West Berlin**: After World War II, Germany was divided into four zones, each zone controlled by one of the main allied powers, the United States, the United Kingdom, France, and the Soviet Union. The city of Berlin was divided in the same manner. In 1949, the zones under control of the Western Allies became the Bundesrepublik Deutschland (BRD), or Federal Republic of Germany (FRG). Shortly after, the Soviet zone became the Deutsche Demokratische Republik (DDR), or German Democratic Republic (GDR). While the Soviet-controlled part of Berlin (East Berlin) served as the GDR's capital, West Berlin received special status, closely linked to the FRG but not fully integrated. While the acronyms BRD and DDR are still widely used in German, FRG and GDR rarely appear in English outside of official documents. Therefore, the more common, if less formal, terms "West Germany" and "East Germany" have been used in this translation in most cases. It is important to note that "West Germany" does not necessarily include "West Berlin."

PREFACE TO THE
ENGLISH-LANGUAGE EDITION

"You have to remain a mole even when many illusions are lost." (Johannes Agnoli, 1990)

W HEN I WROTE THIS BOOK IN THE LATE 1980s, the intention was to present a "short critique" of some of the ideas that circulated within the autonomous movement about its history and organization.

At the time, I was deeply involved in both the radical left wing of the antinuclear movement and the campaign against the 1988 IMF and World Bank Summit in Berlin. I reflected on the understanding of theory and praxis that was associated with the term "autonomous."

Since "Fire and Flames" was a slogan regularly chanted at autonomous demonstrations, I figured it would make a good title for what was meant to be little more than a snapshot of the movement. (The Autonomen wished "Fire and Flames" for the state, of course, not for the homes of asylum seekers—an approach favored by Nazis and racists in the early 1990s, able to conduct their business without state interference.)

Right in time for the legal but "revolutionary" autonomous demonstration on May 1, 1990, in a place once called West Berlin, the first edition of *Feuer und Flamme* appeared. In the following years, the book was hardly reviewed but eagerly read. In 1995, a more concise version was published, on which this translation is based.

The book focuses on the history of the Autonomen in West Germany from 1967 to 1990, the second stage of the Cold War. The era of the Cold War ended with the fall of the Berlin Wall—once, misleadingly, referred to as the "Antifascist Protection Rampart." The instinctive reaction of the Autonomen was charming. During an illegal demonstration on Berlin's Kurfürstendamm they chanted, "In the West They Are Smarter: Their Wall Is Money!" This remains true in the era of the Global War on Terror, announced by the U.S. president after September 11, 2001, with no end in sight. It is an era of crises, catastrophes, and wars. A notion of peace has no place in it. Meanwhile, the persistent calls of reformists to "civilize" capitalism only reveal that we live in the midst of barbarism.

The decision to publish *Feuer und Flamme* under a pseudonym had nothing to do with conspiratorial inclinations. It was a pragmatic way to handle the pretentiousness of an individual to address a phenomenon that many people ought to address—something I still strongly believe! However, the decision also reflects one of the paradoxes of the autonomous movement, namely the unresolved question of hierarchy and leadership. The Autonomen have no *comandantes*, or, to be more precise: they should not have any. At least not in the liberated society in which we, as everyone knows, do not yet live.

Comrade Johannes Agnoli has said something that must be taken very seriously: "The Autonomen do everything wrong, but they give us hope." In fact, despite all the necessary criticism, the Autonomen were a surprisingly refreshing innovation given the situation in West Germany after the end of the 1960s student revolt. The idea and theory of autonomy includes in a formidable manner the practice to reject all notions of order and conformity. This is necessary for self-preservation alone. It also leads to different forms of struggle than, let's say, purely democratic or antifascist approaches.

The principle of autonomy reaches beyond the limits of the organized autonomous movement in Germany, in which it is, in fact, constantly threatened: from the outside by the power of the state, sometimes executed openly, sometimes subtly; and from the inside by narrow-minded cretins who pursue concepts of political identity that entail both authoritarian submission and behavioral therapy. No! In the struggle against social conditions that are neither just nor free, it cannot be right to limit internal organization to "decent behavior" on the grounds of misunderstood immediacy. This, of course, never excludes—rather necessarily includes—help for those who need it!

It remains a challenging task to think and act on the basis of internal contradictions. This is what our comrade Johannes Agnoli has done in his work.

The publication of this book shows that there remains an interest in *Feuer und Flamme*. This gladdens me as much as it reminds me that poverty, unemployment, war, racism, anti-Semitism, ecological destruction, and sexism still need to be replaced by collective happiness and liberation.

The book is illustrated with posters that the "poster digitalizing collective" HKS 13, based in Berlin and Hamburg, collected between 1998 and 2001—HKS 13 stands for the spot color Red. All posters are from West Berlin and West Germany and from the years 1967–90, except for one: the image below was designed by a Paris arts collective in 2001 as a contribution to the antiglobalization protests kicked off by the riots at the 1999 WTO Summit in Seattle. The visual representation of capitalism as a system that has no human face captures the truth. May this realization lead the autonomous movement beyond its own confines and on to a different, a better, life.

Geronimo, Hamburg-Altona, Summer 2011

15

BACKGROUND

THE AUTONOMEN AS THEY EXIST TODAY, in the 1990s, did not exist in the 1950s—neither in the Federal Republic of Germany (FRG) of the "Economic Miracle" [*Wirtschaftswunder*] nor in the Stalinist German Democratic Republic (GDR) of Walter Ulbricht. The Autonomen are a consequence of the uprisings of 1968. These uprisings were mainly carried by the students' movement and spawned a "New Left," developing from a critique both of representative party and trade union politics and of the political concepts of the traditional workers' movement. The critique was directed at Western European Social Democracy, at Eastern European Bolshevism, and even at elements of Southern European anarchism. In contrast both to the capitalist conditions restored in Western Europe after World War II and to the legacy of the traditional workers' movement, the students' movement understood itself as antiauthoritarian. Furthermore, the 1968 uprisings included a rebellion of women against male domination. The critique of "socialist eminences" inspired an autonomous and self-organized women's movement representing a new understanding of the relationship between everyday life, subjectivity, and politics. Last but not least, workers fought militantly against wage labor and capital in the automobile factories with ripple effects all across Europe.

The Autonomen of today can only be understood in the context of the New Left's history, which lasted at least until the end of West Germany in 1989. From a European perspective, the theory and praxis of the West German Autonomen of the 1980s can be seen as a "Second Wave of Autonomous Struggles" after the crushing of the

Italian Autonomia movement in the late 1970s. From a German perspective, the Autonomen can be seen as the next generation of rebels after the 1968 uprisings, a generation that tried to revive the radical dimensions of the political and cultural demands of their forerunners in order to challenge the increasing hypocrisy of the 1968 activists. This also means that the Autonomen carry with them all the shortcomings, losses, and contradictions—but also all the hopes and successes—of over twenty years of radical left and antiparliamentarian politics in West Germany.

The political origins of the Autonomen can be found in currents that became particularly influential after the disintegration of the extraparliamentary opposition [*Außerparlamentarische Opposition*, or APO]: the Spontis, the Italian *operaismo* groups, and the libertarian-anarchist circles of urban subcultures. As these currents began to dissolve in the mid-1970s, parts of the Sponti movement transformed into the German alternative movement. The German Autumn of 1977, a severe state crisis induced by the actions of the Red Army Faction (RAF) with the subsequent death of their imprisoned leadership, further strengthened a widespread skepticism regarding traditional forms of radical organizing. The rejection of cadre groups, an emphasis on the so-called "politics of the first person," direct action, direct democracy, and the establishment of a "counter public" [*Gegenöffentlichkeit*] were pillars of the New Social Movements.

The rise of these movements coincided in the 1970s with the decline of the Marxist-Leninist K-groups that had emerged as a result of the 1968 uprisings. The rejection of K-group politics was an important part of the self-identification and praxis of many antiauthoritarian activists of the 1970s: "Due to the emergence of the Spontis and the 'Urban Indians' in West Germany in the mid-1970s, the notion of 'autonomy' became increasingly important in the cultural and political scene. Publications that were central for these discussions were West Berlin's *Info-BUG/Bug-Info*, Frankfurt's *Informations-Dienst*, and *Autonomie. Materialen gegen die Fabriksgesellschaft*. We find the beginnings of an independent autonomous movement around 1980" (M. Manrique).

It can be said that the autonomous movement formed as a radical and militant wing within the New Social Movements. Despite historical links to the 1968 uprisings, there were hardly any personal connections and many autonomous activists seemed to be unaware of the history their own movement built on. The purpose of this book is therefore to draw a historical sketch. The term "autonomy" will not be examined in depth. Nonetheless, here are a few introductory comments:

Two hundred years ago, the term "autonomy" was already analyzed by fellows like Immanuel Kant and Georg Wilhelm Friedrich Hegel, shining lights of bourgeois enlightenment. Did I know anything about this in the 1980s? No. My curiosity at the time was, unfortunately, not great enough to take me back that far in history. I am including the information, however, to illustrate that the term "autonomy" would eventually deserve more exhaustive study. In its everyday usage, it has been reduced to little more than a synonym for "independence." But constantly stressing the importance of something as vague as "independence"—without ever clarifying what it is that we want to be independent from, and why—is a rather hollow and flimsy venture. Today, at the threshold to the twenty-first century, we are more reliant on other people than ever in history and hence also more dependent. To ignore this when praising "autonomy" and to nurture an uncritical cult of "independence" only reproduces bourgeois ideology and egotistical values. It reflects social interaction that serves capitalism—and not just in an abstract manner! In fact, the uncritical embrace of "independence" has led to behavior within the autonomous movement that has done much harm within its ranks.

Bodo Schulze provides an interesting definition of "autonomy": "'Autonomy' is a fragile thing. Or rather: autonomy is no thing at all. It stands for a certain form of relationship between people who associate in order to destroy all forms of oppression. It is a relationship that cannot be grasped theoretically. Theories can only be formulated about phenomena that exist in and by themselves. 'Autonomy' only exists when people start to be active revolutionaries."

Sometimes, the notion of "autonomy" is seen as an "Italian export product" with an originally "proletarian character" that was transformed into a "characteristically German form: petty-bourgeois and individualistic." Is this true?

Maybe the definition of "autonomy" by Johannes Agnoli can help us here. It is based on radical experiences in both Italy and West Germany in the mid-1970s:

> The autonomy I mean is class autonomy. . . . This form of autonomy has two meanings: First, it is a class movement, a movement of labor against capital, a movement of workers as subjects of production against workers as objects of valorization. At the same time, autonomy goes beyond the

> workplace: it describes a mass movement against the capi-
> talist reduction of everyone to consumer objects. In both
> cases, autonomy means an attempt to free oneself from the
> logic of capital. . . . Autonomy does not mean to reject the
> principle of organization. It means to reject a certain form
> of organization: a form that prioritizes the interests of the
> organization over the interests of the class.

Whether we want to adopt this definition or not, we have to be aware of one thing: many formerly and currently active comrades have a tendency to generalize their own experiences. It is a way to give one's own activism particular meaning—at least in hindsight. It might allow some comrades to flatter themselves, but there is no reason why others have to agree with them. Let us take those as an example who stress the Italian origins of the autonomous movement. Are these really the only origins that matter for the autonomous movement in Germany? Is this movement not equally rooted in domestic developments of the 1950s and 1960s, even if it the term was not used at the time? We can recall the "lumpenproletariat riots" at 1950s rock concerts, the so-called Schwabing Riots of 1962 in Munich, or the heroics of Subversive Aktion [an eccentric activist group] in the mid-1960s. All of these examples suggest that the specter of autonomy in Germany has not simply been imported from Italy and that it is much older than often assumed. Indeed, it seems that autonomous politics have caused headaches and sleepless nights for the powerful for quite some time. In any case, the contemporary history of the Autonomen starts at the latest with the political debates and conflicts of the late 1960s.

Another difficulty in describing the Autonomen derives from the rather random usage of terms such as "autonomous movement," "left-wing radicalism," or "political power of the Autonomen." This is one more reason why I will abstain from a static definition of "autonomy" and of the "autonomous movement." The Autonomen are a diverse and shifting phenomenon and any static definition would appear both random and authoritarian. Furthermore, the radical left of the 1970s and 1980s never had a common platform, neither in the form of a publication nor of an organization. It entailed many spontaneous, in-dividualistic, and anarchistic moments that make it difficult to suggest a chronological history. Comrades had better things to do than amass reports of their actions in folders. Furthermore, many left the scene, while others moved from project to project. However, while this makes writing the movement's history difficult, it also means that the move-ment is blessed with a wide variety of initiatives and approaches that do not allow its instrumentalization by the established political powers. In conclusion, we can state that the radical currents of the 1960s and 1970s that would eventually lead to the Autonomen were as clearly distinct from the traditional organizations of the workers' movement as they differed from the traditional forms and theories of anarchism.

To give this book at least some kind of structure, it has been divided into three blocks: the 1968 revolt, the 1970s, and the 1980s. These categories are, of course, simplified and the lines between them far from clear. However, I hope they can provide a framework that will make it easier for readers to understand the connections between certain developments in a wider context. Everything in this book is interrelated.

I. THE EMERGENCE OF AUTONOMOUS POLITICS IN WEST GERMANY

A TASTE OF REVOLUTION: 1968

"The material conditions for the realization of our destiny exist today. The development of the productive forces has reached a point that makes the end of hunger, war, and domination materially possible. All depends on the conscious will of the people to make their own history . . ." (Rudi Dutschke, June 1967)

THE YEAR OF 1968 MARKS AN important rupture in post–World War II history, both in West Germany and internationally. In 1966–67, West Germany went through a massive economic crisis when the so-called Economic Miracle ended. On the parliamentary level, the SPD and the CDU formed a coalition government. Together, they prepared an "emergency constitution," which, in case of a "state of crisis," would allow the suspension of all civil liberties and the implementation of an "emergency government" no longer controlled by parliament. The left-liberal public, trade unions, and students saw this as a frightening step toward an "authoritarian state": a "democracy" without democrats and without opposition.

Internationally, the year of 1968 was characterized by important political developments and strong student movements: in the United States, Italy, France, Spain, the Netherlands, Mexico, Japan, etc. The April 1968 Tet Offensive by the Vietcong against the U.S. imperialists challenged the worldwide belief in the invincibility of U.S. power and leadership. The events of May 1968 in Paris, with barricades and fights in the inner city, brought the bourgeois capitalist system in

France to the brink of collapse. At the same time, the Prague Spring kindled hopes of a "socialism with a human face."

In this historical context, the West German student movement and the extraparliamentary opposition understood themselves as a part of an international revolutionary uprising.

The Student Revolt

In the early 1960s, the Sozialistische Deutsche Studentenbund (SDS) found it difficult to organize among the mostly complacent and conservative students. The SDS had been expelled by the SPD in 1961 for refusing to follow the party's complete integration into the bourgeois social and political system. Subsequently, the SDS became a gathering place for disillusioned left intellectuals from West Germany and West Berlin.

In the mid-1960s, the development of Marxist theory, the democratization of the universities, and internationalist solidarity were the priorities of the SDS. After the Algerian liberation struggle had been the international focus in the late 1950s, Algerian independence meant that other liberation struggles became increasingly important, particularly the one in Vietnam. In West Berlin, the SDS organized their first public international solidarity actions. New protest forms were developed that differed significantly from the ritualized "funeral marches" of the Adenauer era [German chancellor from 1949 to 1963] and turned protests into spaces of actual resistance and adventure. Rudi Dutschke, one of the most prominent SDS figures, propagated illegal mass action as a necessary means for individual and collective transformation. Students engaged poorly prepared police units in street-fights and turned into the prime enemy of the powerful and reactionary Springer media empire.

The developments in West Berlin came to a head when the shah of Iran, Reza Pahlavi, arrived for an official visit on June 2, 1967. Consistent with its internationalist commitments, the SDS organized protests against the reception of a mass murderer by German authorities. For the first time in the history of West Germany and West Berlin, the state security agencies engaged in an "emergency operation." More than ten thousand police were called in to protect the honorary guest, and several highways were closed off to guarantee the shah's safe passage.

On June 2, two thousand people protested rather peacefully in front of the German Opera. Most of them were high school and university students that had been mobilized by SDS events at the Free University about the Iranian dictatorship. The protesters received the shah with chants of "Murderer," smoke bombs, and eggs. In response, they were first attacked by steel-bar-wielding Iranian secret service agents and then by German police, which brutally dissolved the protest. In the course of the events, the student Benno Ohnesorg was fatally shot in the back of the head. When false rumors started spreading about a police officer having been killed by a protester, the Berlin Senate declared a general ban on demonstrations in the entire city. The hostility toward the oppositional students, fueled by the state authorities and the Springer press, reached unprecedented heights.

The students installed their own investigative committee and disclosed the truth about the actions of the police and the death of Benno Ohnesorg. They formed council-like structures that organized numerous information events and managed—at least for some days—to create a counterdiscourse that challenged the state's strategies of exclusion and repression. The experiences with the Springer press led to the first discussions of direct action within the SDS and to a campaign under the slogan "Expropriate Springer."

The Student Revolt and the Extraparliamentary Opposition

Until 1967, the student movement was concentrated in West Berlin. It only spread to West Germany in 1968. That year marked both the peak of the movement—which had turned into a broad extraparliamentary opposition movement—and its demise.

In February, the "International Congress on Vietnam" gathered several thousand participants at the main lecture hall of the Berlin Institute of Technology. It was the zenith of years of internationalist solidarity work by the SDS and of support for the Vietnamese resistance struggle. One of the main efforts of the SDS was to counteract the propaganda of the West German media and to spread its own information about U.S. imperialism and the situation in Vietnam. At the congress, the SDS was perceived as a part of a worldwide revolutionary struggle that linked anti-imperialist liberation struggles in the "Third World" with socialist struggles in the industrialized nations. A common final resolution, adopted on February 17, stated that "the political opposition in this country is entering the transition from protest to resistance." It was discussed to provide supplies for the Vietnamese resistance and to sabotage U.S. Army facilities. As a long-term perspective, "Crush NATO" was proclaimed. The congress ended with an internationalist demonstration of more than ten thousand people. For the first time after Berlin's partition, the streets of the Western part were filled with red flags. Many protesters formed chains by linking their arms, inspired by France's Gauche Prolétarienne.

On April 11, there was an assassination attempt on Rudi Dutschke. It followed months of defamation against Dutschke by the Springer press. During the following Easter holidays, West Berlin and West Germany saw the heaviest street-fighting in their history, especially

INTERNATIONALE VIETNAM-KONFERENZ WESTBERLIN
Koordinierung anti-imperialistischer Aktionen in Westeuropa

17. Februar 1968, 11.oo Uhr, Auditorium Maximum der TU

DER KAMPF DES VIETNAMESISCHEN VOLKES UND DIE GLOBALSTRATEGIE DES IMPERIALISMUS

Forum I   Die vietnamesische Revolution
Forum II   Vietnam und die Revolution in der Dritten Welt
Forum III   Der anti-imperialistische und anti-kapitalisti-
             sche Kampf in den kapitalistischen Ländern

Sozialistischer Deutscher Studentenbund

18. Februar 1968, 1
vom Rathaus Sch

GROSSKUNDGEBUNG mit

S. de Beauvoir (Frankreich), D. Dillinger (USA), R. Dutschke (SDS), C. L. Guggomos (Kampagne für Demokratie und
Abrüstung), Melva Hernandez (ZK der KP Kuba), E. Mandel
(Belgien), D. Smith (Black Power SNNC, USA), Peter Weiss
und Vertretern der FNL

Sozialistischer Deutscher Studentenbund
Kampagne für Demokratie und Abrüstung (Regional-Aus-
schuß Berlin)

"FOR THE VICTORY OF THE VIETNAMESE REVOLUTION:
IT IS EVERY REVOLUTIONARY'S DUTY TO MAKE THE REVOLUTION"

at barricades erected at Springer printing plants. In West Berlin, two thousand protesters tried to storm the Springer headquarters. Several delivery vans were set on fire. All in all, sixty thousand people partook in the protests, twenty-one thousand police were on duty, and over one thousand people were arrested.

The high number of protesters fuelled further discussions about the relationship between protest and resistance. In the May issue of the left-wing journal *Konkret*, Ulrike Meinhof wrote: "To protest means to state that you dislike something. To resist means to make sure that what you dislike disappears. . . . During the Easter holidays, the line between verbal protest and physical resistance was crossed."

The Springer protests did not only involve university students but also high school students and young workers. For the first time, stronger links were created between the revolting students and other social groups. This was confirmed on May 1, 1968, when in West Berlin and various West German cities APO protests were organized next to the official May events of the Confederation of German Trade Unions, DGB. In West Berlin, forty thousand people joined the APO march. However, the political ties between the students and sections of the working class were short-lived. They could not be sustained during the fight against the provision of emergency laws. While "Emergency and Democracy"— a broad coalition of unionists, intellectuals, student representatives, and even individual SPD members—managed to mobilize sixty thousand people for a "March on Bonn" on May 11, the students' demand for a general strike was rejected by the workers' movement; only a few regional warning strikes could be organized. Despite strong student agitation outside the factories—inspired by the events in France—no close collaboration between students and workers could ever be established. Unlike in France and Italy, there were no revolutionary groups that the workers had formed themselves and it was difficult for the extraparliamentary opposition to gain a foothold in the factories. In the following years, the difficulties in working-class mobilization led to a variety of different strategies within the German New Left.

The Politics of the SDS

From 1965 to 1969, the discussions within the SDS consisted mainly of exchanges between the centers of SDS activism, namely West Berlin and Frankfurt, on the one hand, and "provincial" SDS towns like Hamburg, Kiel, Cologne, Marburg, Heidelberg, Tübingen, and Munich, on the other. Politically, the central line of conflict ran between the "traditionalists" and the "antiauthoritarians."

The "traditionalists" included all currents that followed the orthodox communist wing of the workers' movement. When, in September 1968, the Deutsche Kommunistische Partei (DKP) was founded, a successor to the old Communist Party of Germany, KPD, banned in 1956, practically the entire SDS groups of Marburg and Cologne joined.

The "antiauthoritarians," on the other hand, rooted themselves strongly in critical theory, left communism, and anarchist critiques of Marxism. This meant not simply digging out marginalized elements of the German workers' movement's history. At numerous congresses and teach-ins, the antiauthoritarians developed new theoretical approaches and laid the foundation for a new political praxis. Theory took on the form of a tool shed, with practical usefulness as the main criterion and plenty of room for improvisation. To provoke social tension was more important than dogmatic doctrine.

The best-known speakers of the antiauthoritarians were Rudi Dutschke (SDS Berlin) and Hans-Jürgen Krahl (SDS Frankfurt). Dutschke's ideas were strongly influenced by the Situationist International. He had joined the SDS in the mid-1960s as a member of the group Subversive Aktion. Krahl's ideas were based on his discussions with Horkheimer and Adorno at Frankfurt's Institute of Social Research.

Popular expressions of the antiauthoritarian tendency were the actions of Berlin's Kommune 1. Its members practiced provocative forms of communal living, ridiculed Free University professors as "narrow-minded fools," attacked the U.S. vice president with pudding, threw paint bombs, distributed flyers that called for the burning of shopping centers, and staged "Moabit Soap Operas" that ridiculed the courts [many political trials were held in the Berlin suburb of Moabit, also home to a notorious prison]. The politics of the Kommune 1 were a permanent call to action, not only to fight the state and society, but also to change oneself. Eventually, the Kommune 1 members were expelled by the SDS Berlin. Traditionalists, in their characteristic "objective rationality," accused them of "voluntarism, escapism, and pretense" (Mosler).

However, the antiauthoritarian positions of Dutschke and Krahl prevailed at the Twenty-Second Delegates' Conference of the SDS in Frankfurt in September 1967. They stated in their common presentation: "Many SDS comrades are no longer willing to accept notions of abstract socialism that have nothing to do with their daily lives. . . . Being rejected within one's own institutional milieu demands a guerrilla mentality if we do not want assimilation and cynicism to be the next steps."

In the wake of the conference, antiauthoritarian notions of "Here and Now" and of Herbert Marcuse's "Great Refusal" dominated the actions of the student movement and the extraparliamentary opposition. It proved difficult, though, to organize on this basis. The vagueness of the antiauthoritarian current reflected the origins of the student revolt. A lack of political clarity was common within the left. Sometimes it was little more than a diffuse but very compelling idea of emancipation that drew people to the streets and barricades.

The limits of the APO's mobilizing potential became evident in the anti-Springer actions of May 1, 1968, and in the fight against the emergency laws. At the same time, the SDS started to break apart and was no longer able to formulate any convincing orientation and strategy.

In early November, following a court case against a radical lawyer, one thousand APO activists won a street-fight against the police in West Berlin. The "Battle of the Tegeler Weg" was seen by many as a night of revenge for the brutality they had suffered at the hands of the police during many years. However, the militant confrontation with the state could not provide any political perspectives.

The Demise of the SDS

At the 1968 SDS Delegates' Conference in Hanover, the increasing ideological divisions within the organization made constructive debate impossible. Especially in the traditional centers of the APO, West Berlin and Frankfurt, second-tier SDS members demanded a solution to the organizational crisis. Addresses by factions of the SDS Berlin and the SDS Heidelberg already outlined the programs of the future K-groups Kommunistische Partei Deutschlands–Aufbauorganisation

(KPD-AO) and Kommunistischer Bund Westdeutschland (KBW). The concepts were heavily criticized by the antiauthoritarians (Krahl: "The SDS does not stand in the tradition of the communist workers' parties!"), but dissolution could no longer be prevented. Under the impression of workers' strikes in September 1969, the Marxist-Leninist party concepts had become compelling for many radical students. Revolutionary parties were considered the necessary means to achieve real social transformation in West Germany.

In West Berlin, the radical movement disintegrated extremely fast. Hardly any of the grassroots committees founded by the APO in 1968—in universities, high schools, factories, and neighborhoods—still existed, especially in the area of production. Most student activists shied away from the "tedious" daily work in the factories. Eventually, this caused deep alienation between the university and the factory committees, which led to different APO factions and the formation of cadres. The attempt to reestablish a common platform at a conference in late 1969 failed.

Eventually, the traditionalist current of the SDS became basically absorbed by the DKP, while the antiauthoritarian camp was deeply divided—some left their antiauthoritarian convictions behind and founded Maoist and even Stalinist parties, others continued to eschew all forms of centralist and dogmatic organization. The situation was further complicated by SDS women founding their own independent organization and forming the basis for the emerging autonomous women's movement.

Militant Grassroots Currents

Several grassroots currents were part of the uprisings of the late 1960s but never connected to the SDS. They consisted mainly of independent university students, high school students, apprentices, and young workers. They were militant and mainly operated on the street:

> The grassroots currents had many names and could be found in many places: drifting hash rebels in West Berlin, Black Panther Committees around Frankfurt, White Rose and deserter groups around Hamburg and Hanover, the Socialist Patients' Collective in Heidelberg. Their actions were diverse as well: supporting deserted GIs and German

soldiers, attacking facilities of the Allies, engaging in direct action against reformatories, prisons, and psychiatric institutions, sabotaging arms production for the Portuguese colonial regime, removing files from diplomatic missions of state terrorists, stealing and publishing secret documents, interfering with the investigative apparatus of the police, arranging money for alternative projects (K.H. Roth).

The grassroots currents represented most clearly the "spirit of subversion" within the APO. They attacked "German diligence" and "German work ethics," and many comrades rejected the idea of a professional career and lifelong submission to the system. The open contempt for "achievement" was a central part of the '68 movement.

What Did '68 Mean?

The student revolt broke the rigid anticommunist consensus that had characterized West Germany since the end of World War II. Direct action and education about social coercion undermined the pillars of the country's late-capitalist system. It also made the ongoing class differences obvious that had been hidden by the ideology of the Economic Miracle.

The revolt brought a new, uncompromising political morality. Its protagonists rebelled against a generation that portrayed itself as an unaware victim of history while carrying the responsibility for Auschwitz. The new generation intended to make history as conscious subjects, thereby changing everyday life. They made the continuity of fascism in West Germany a public issue.

The 1968 revolt brought new questions and demands for West Germany and West Berlin. It "articulated a cultural discomfort, it disclosed collective processes of repression, it demanded political ethics, and it criticized repressive sexuality as much as the norms of a consumer and performance society" (Kraushaar).

At its height, in the spring and summer of 1968, the revolt spread from the universities to other social areas and merged with subversive sentiments of working-class youth. At its best, the 1968 revolt was a combination of anti-imperialist, anticapitalist, and countercultural elements that constituted a radical opposition to the existing order of West Berlin and West Germany.

LA SOLA SOLUZIONE
LA RIVOLUZIONE:
ITALY'S AUTONOMIA MOVEMENT

THE CONCEPT OF "AUTONOMOUS POLITICS," as we know it in Germany today, has without doubt been influenced by the student, workers', and youth revolts of the 1960s and 1970s in Italy. The so-called Autonomia movement consisted of subversive and militant activities in factory and neighborhood struggles that were organized independently from the traditional workers' organizations. Especially in Northern Italy, the actions of students and militant workers formed a common struggle. Radical German APO activists began to follow these developments closely.

What Happened in Italy in the 1960s?

The revolting Italian workers and students of the late 1960s faced entirely different social conditions than the workers and students in Germany. Italy was the weakest member of the European Economic Community. It was on Europe's periphery. In the international division of labor, Italy played no significant role. Furthermore, the country was structurally divided into two parts: the North was characterized by economic development based on modern capitalist production and workers' organizations, while the South remained deeply agricultural and partly feudal.

The Italian class struggles were a joint effort of students and mostly unskilled assembly line workers from the big factories. They were conceptualized theoretically by unionists and left-wing intellectuals aligned with the Italian Communist Party, PCI, and the Italian Socialist Party, PSI. Of particular importance was the work of people like Raniero Panzieri, Mario Tronti, Romano Alquati, and Toni Negri. Most of their texts were originally published in the journal *Quaderni Rossi* (1961–64), and then, after a split, in the journal *Classe Operaia*, which existed until 1967.

After failed attempts in the late 1950s to rejuvenate the PCI and the PSI, the mentioned intellectuals focused their critique on the official institutions of the workers' movement and emphasized the potentials of extrainstitutional political organizing. In late 1959, Panziere left the PSI headquarters in Rome for Turin in order "to revisit the working class in the factories" (Rieland). In 1962, militant clashes between thousands of FIAT workers and the police around Turin's Piazza Statuto lasted for several days. Panzieri and his allies saw this as a confirmation for their prediction of an impending class struggle that was not interested in reformist mediation by the traditional workers' organizations. Indeed, the riots of the workers, which followed the signing of a collective labor agreement, were not backed by the industrial unions. This only deepened the rift between the workers and their official representatives. The struggles revealed a new type of laborer who no longer carried the characteristics of the old skilled worker. Most of the protesters were unskilled assembly line workers who had recently migrated to Italy's North from the South. The clashes on the Piazza Statuto manifested a transformation within the Italian working class.

From Marxism to Operaismo

The developments in Italy led to a reevaluation and an ever-increasing critique of orthodox Marxism, which had long dominated the Italian communist movement. New readings of *Das Kapital* and *Grundrisse* were used to challenge the claims of the PCI, the PSI, and the trade unions to carry the workers' struggle. The focus shifted from organizations that worked as mediators in political struggles to the subjects of the political struggles themselves: the workers in the factories and in their neighborhoods. The school of Marxism that developed became known as *operaismo*, at the time the most radical left-wing critique of Marxism's orthodox interpretations.

Operaismo revealed the violence of everyday capitalism in the factories and in the neighborhoods. It was not interested in integrating the working class into capitalist development, the approach favored by the traditional workers' organizations. In operaismo, the precondition for a truly socialist society was the complete negation of the existing system. The operaists proposed a "strategic reversal" within Marxism. It was not the development of capital that determined capitalism but the development of the working class. Revolutionary strategy could therefore only be based on the "subjective factor" of the proletariat, since the labor force was the only aspect of capitalist development that was not controllable. In short, capitalism could only be overcome by the conscious action of the workers.

For the operaists, the main revolutionary protagonist was no longer the skilled worker but the unskilled mass worker of the assembly line [operaio massa]. They demanded that the workers directly take control of the labor process in the factories. This was considered the central tool for revolutionary social change. In the revolts of 1968–69, the theoretical approach of the operaists corresponded to the everyday experiences of assembly line workers in the big factories. Unprecedented forms of factory and neighborhood struggles were the consequence, also because of Italy's particular social conditions: among others, the North-South conflict, a deeply rooted tradition of militant and armed resistance against fascism, and a strong communist party.

Especially in the FIAT factories—the "heart of Italian capitalism"—the assembly line worker was little more than a small accessory in the gigantic machinery of mass production. The monotony of executing the most primitive tasks without end led many workers to social and psychological exhaustion. Labor as productive activity had ceased to exist. The rage of the workers was no longer directed at capitalist control over the means of production alone but also at the organization of labor. At times, the traditional workers' organizations lost all control over the revolting assembly line workers who organized in grassroots committees springing up everywhere. Delegates with imperative mandates were sent to big workers' assemblies. The workers' actions were characterized by great flexibility, unpredictability, and militancy: there were wildcat strikes that, in combination with effective sabotage, managed to paralyze wide areas of production. There was also widespread absenteeism in the factories. The struggles peaked in the fall of 1969 when, during wage disputes, workers went on general strike nationwide and a solidarity demonstration in Turin gathered six hundred thousand metal workers.

From *Operaio Massa* to *Operaio Sociale*

Eventually, the traditional trade unions managed to reintegrate the autonomous workers' movement through a change of union politics. Many grassroots committees were incorporated into the union structure on the lowest level. Partly, this was a consequence of the leadership vacuum within the autonomous workers' movement in the fall of 1969. This allowed the traditional unions to gain a foothold in the autonomous struggles. In 1970, the PCI campaigned under the slogan, "From the Struggle in the Factories to the Struggle for Reforms."

Clashes continued in the North Italian factories, but the militancy was past its peak. The ruling class had created a reactionary climate in the country, blatantly blaming the actions of secret service agents on the autonomous left—for example, a bombing that left sixteen people dead in a Milan bank in late 1969. This strategy united different groups of Italy's diverse social strata in their opposition to the revolutionaries: the unemployed of Southern Italy, small farmers, the rural proletariat, the urban middle class, and others.

Despite the reactionary backlash, the autonomous workers' movement still controlled parts of the production process in the big factories. This led to targeted campaigns of several years that aimed at decentralizing the production process to undermine the autonomous workers' influence.

In 1973, Potere Operaio, the biggest of the militant workers' groups of the 1960s disbanded. It was no longer able to develop an effective response to the new strategies of capital. FIAT had initiated massive restructuring which met little resistance within the factories as it happened outside of the area of production. The company developed industrial robots and outsourced as well as diversified the production process. These measures undermined the power of the workers where they had been strongest: the workplace.

The process of decentralization and automation led to a drastic reduction of jobs in the formal sector and to an enormous expansion of production in small factories and at home. Theorists like Negri described this development using the term *Fabbrica diffusa*. This included the immense growth of a "marginal proletariat," which became an important factor in the Italian economy and in Italian politics. In the late 1970s, the marginal proletariat was estimated at about nine million people. It was mainly composed of youths and by sick and old workers who had lost steady employment due to the decentralization process. They only got part-time contracts and were regularly laid off and therefore dependent on state subsidies. In addition, there were tens of thousands of students and academics who, after the educational boom of the 1960s, entered labor markets that had long been saturated, for example, in state bureaucracy. There was simply no work for many university graduates.

The operaists who were still aiming for a revolutionary organization of the proletariat apart from the traditional workers' organizations shifted its focus from the *operaio massa*, the "worker of mass production" of the 1960s, to the *operaio sociale*, the "worker of the social field." This expanded the struggle to areas outside of the immediate workplace. It was a reaction not only to the decentralization of the production process but also to the women's and youth movements.

The Autonomia Movement of 1977

In 1977, the Autonomia movement experienced a second wave. It was now carried by the marginal proletariat consisting of students, unemployed youth, and precarious laborers who joined remaining elements of the Autonomia movement of the 1960s. The second wave of Autonomia was even more anti-institutional than the first and developed a biting critique of the PCI. In 1977, there was a wide range of creative and militant protests directed at the state. The centers of the revolt were the universities and the big cities in the North.

The movement consisted of two main currents: Autonomia Creativa, very similar to the German Spontis in challenging conventional forms of politics and embracing riots as happenings, and Autonomia Operaia Organizzata, the attempt to transform spontaneous revolt into a continuous attack on the capitalist system by means of organizing.

Furthermore, Autonomia Creativa was divided into two main groups: the Circoli del Proletario Giovanile, the "Circles of Young Workers," and the Indiani Metropolitani, the "Urban Indians." The Circles of Young Workers had begun to form in 1975 as a spontaneous and loose form of youth organization in neighborhoods most strongly affected by economic marginalization. They propagated the immediate recuperation of their lives, which stood in sharp contrast to the PCI's support of austerity measures, moral rigidity, and personal frugality. The youths went on collective "proletarian shopping" sprees, that is, they looted supermarkets. They also occupied government-run youth centers and transformed them into self-managed meeting spaces, they fought against hard drugs and heroin dealers undermining their social structures, they rode public transport for free, and they refused to pay for rock concerts and movie screenings. The most spectacular action by the Young Workers was the storming of Milan's La Scala in December 1976, which ended with several thousand proletarian youths looting luxury shops in the city center. Meanwhile, the Urban Indians were mainly active in university towns. The reference to indigenous people stood for a radical rejection of urban and capitalist life. The Urban Indians propagated alternative values (ecological awareness, vegetarianism, sexual liberation), negated instrumental reason, and celebrated the liberating dimensions of hashish.

Autonomia Creativa circles published hundreds of alternative journals and ran more than fifty radical radio stations, Radio Alice in Bologna being the best known. Activists painted murals, performed street theater, and organized festivals. The notion of creating "free spaces" in order to politicize everyday life and to satisfy needs in collective self-determination was central. The image of the Urban Indian was enthusiastically adapted by many German Spontis.

Autonomia Operaia Organizzata, on the other hand, saw such tendencies as attempts to escape the system rather than to destroy it. This current consisted of a number of loosely coordinated committees and collectives, which also included remnants of the 1969 grassroots factory committees—for example, members of the group Potere Operaio who had started to shift their activism away from the factories in 1973.

In early 1977, the new movement exploded. Triggered by the abolition of some holidays and by plans for conservative reforms in higher learning, students in Palermo, Catania, and Naples occupied universities. The movement quickly spread across the country. After an armed fascist attack on a general assembly at the University of Rome on February 1, thousands of students took to the streets and were attacked by police with pistols and machine guns. For the first time, protesters also used guns—a phenomenon that became increasingly common during the following months. The P38 turned into a symbol for the movement.

After the demonstration in Rome, the university was occupied. On February 17, the rupture between the traditional workers' organizations and the Autonomia movement became more apparent than ever: when the chairman of the communist trade union wanted to give a speech at the university, he was jeered by four to five thousand youths. Fights erupted between the union's security forces and the students during his speech, in which he criticized the students' "welfare ideology" and their "parasitism at the cost of productive labor." The students perceived this as cynical given the situation most of them were in. Eventually, they—literally—kicked the "fat cat" Lama out of the university and celebrated the event as the "Piazza Statuto of the Operaio Sociale."

Different protests followed in rapid succession. In Bologna, once the shining example of communist city administration, numerous buildings were squatted, restaurants looted, cinemas occupied, etc. The situation escalated on March 11 when police killed an autonomous activist on the university campus. Days of rioting followed and a gun shop was looted. Students managed to keep the police away from the old town for three days after barricading it strategically. It needed the Italian Army to retake it.

On March 12, fifty thousand people joined a demonstration in Rome to protest the sentencing of an anarchist. The demonstration turned into one of the biggest street-fights that the Italian capital ever saw. Groups of the Autonomia Operaia Organizzata delivered on their threat of a "new level of confrontation": two gun shops were looted, numerous shops, cafés, and hotels ravaged, and hundreds of cars and buses toppled and torched. Offices and newspapers outlets of the Christian Democratic Party were attacked with petrol bombs.

The demonstration marked a turning point in the development of the Autonomia movement. Many protesters were not prepared for the high level of militancy but had to bear the brunt of police retaliation. The situation escalated further on May 14 during a demonstration in Milan. Groups of armed youths attacked the police and killed one officer. This led to the increased isolation of the Autonomia Operaia Organizzata within the Italian left. Not much solidarity was forthcoming during the wave of state repression that followed. At the same time, the Autonomia Creativa retreated into drug-fuelled urban subculture, rural communes, or the Italian Radical Party, comparable to the German Greens.

More than three hundred autonomous activists were imprisoned by the summer of 1977. The arrests were actively supported by the PCI that had published names of autonomous "ringleaders" in its papers. Bologna's Radio Alice was banned and its equipment confiscated. The state targeted the infrastructure of the movement: bookstores, publishing houses, newspaper offices, etc. All of these measures were justified by an alleged "subversive association" conspiring to bring down the Italian state.

Parts of the Autonomia Operaia Organizzata tried to prevent the complete dissolution of the movement by increasing militant action even further [*Guerriglia diffusa*]. A violent challenge to the state apparatus was seen as the only option to unfold a revolutionary process. "General assemblies must go underground!" However, this did little to stop the increased alienation of the activists from the masses.

On April 7, 1979, the state struck its final blow, arresting hundreds more associated with the Autonomia Operaia Organizzata, including Toni Negri. Of the four thousand political prisoners in Italy in 1981, more than one thousand belonged to this group. April 7, 1979, marked a strategic defeat for the Autonomia Operaia Organizzata, from which it could not recover.

Despite its demise, operaismo played a significant role for the identity of the German autonomous left. Almost all of its key texts had been translated into German during the 1970s. The challenge was to turn the theoretical concepts into viable political praxis.

LEFT RADICALISM
IN THE 1970S

IN WEST GERMANY, THE YEARS FROM 1969 to 1973 marked the period of "reform euphoria" and of the "peace chancellor," Willy Brandt, who pursued a new politics with respect to the Eastern European bloc. The Jusos, the SPD's youth organization, gained one hundred thousand new members. They practiced a "double strategy" with respect to social conflict in West Germany and co-opted various grassroots initiatives.

Toward the end of the student revolt, the nonorganized antiauthoritarians were one of the main currents of the radical left, next to the Jusos, the DKP, and the K-groups. The antiauthoritarian groups were united in a rejection of all "vanguards" and the notion of "leadership." Their political praxis aimed at a "politicization of everyday life." Outside of the universities, the antiauthoritarians were active in self-managed kindergartens, autonomous youth centers, self-help groups, neighborhood initiatives, and solidarity groups for marginalized communities.

In West Berlin, the main journal of the militant grassroots currents between 1969 and 1972 was the *883*. It was the voice of the city's militant subculture, the so-called Blues Scene. The Blues Scene's activities reached from attacks on banks and the foundation of housing cooperatives to protests outside reformatories and "smoke-ins."

The *883* became a strong critic of the Marxist-Leninist KPD-AO (A-zero in the jargon of many), which played a dominant role in the city's radical left. Clandestine organization was seen as a practical antiauthoritarian and militant alternative to dogmatic party concepts, and several *883* editors and contributors went underground, including Georg von Rauch, Tommie Weisbecker, Holger Meins, Werner Sauber, and Peter Paul Zahl. This step was not representative of the majority of antiauthoritarian activists in the early 1970s, though.

The terms *Sponti* and *Anarcho* emerged around 1970 as names for rather informal political groups that mainly gathered in their respective neighborhoods. In West Berlin, the Proletarische Linke/ Parteiinitiative (PL/PI) managed to combine Leninist propaganda with Sponti activism and for a short period (1971–72) had many sympathizers among nonorganized activists. In 1973, some comrades left the universities to organize in districts like Kreuzberg and Wedding. These circles founded the Info-BUG (Info Berliner Undogmatischer Gruppen) in 1974, which served as the Spontis' main publication until the late 1970s.

The following chapters describe the attempts of the radical left of the 1970s to contribute politically, practically, socially, and theoretically to social change in West Germany. All of the approaches presented were, in some way, influential for the Autonomen of the 1980s.

"We Want Everything!":
Grassroots Organizing in the Factories

One of the Sponti currents of the German radical left of the early 1970s was strongly inspired by the struggles in Italy. The forming of operaist groups in West Germany coincided with "the demise of the extraparliamentary opposition and the emergence of the K-groups" (Bierbrauer). Operaist theory provided liberation from dogmatic interpretations of Marxism. Operaismo's main appeal was viewing the working class as the subject of its history rather than as a victim of historical circumstances.

In several West German cities, so-called Workplace Project Groups [*Betriebsprojektgruppen*] were formed that operated under names like Arbeiterkampf [Workers' Struggle] in Cologne, Revolutionärer Kampf [Revolutionary Struggle] in Frankfurt, Arbeitersache [The Worker's Cause] in Munich, and Proletarische Front [Proletarian Front] in Hamburg and Bremen, in order to discuss the possibilities of political interventions in factories and neighborhoods. Some groups also made the step from discussion to praxis.

While the Marxist-Leninists simply entered the factories with a conventional interpretation of the working class, the operaist groups understood that the transformation of a student revolt into a workers' struggle implied a number of challenges. They insisted on first collecting experience in and from the factories, since the forms of organization, strategy, and tactics of the factory struggle could not be based on orthodox Marxist interpretations. In the beginning, the political intervention in the factories was first and foremost a "means of study," where activism should help reveal the actual consciousness of the workers. From February 1973 until the end of the summer of 1975, the Workplace Project Groups issued a common paper, *Wir wollen alles* ["We want everything"]. The groups' common ground was defined by Munich's Arbeitersache as follows: "Workers' autonomy; focus on practical factory work; radical trade union critique; integration of migrant workers in the domestic struggle; practical relation to everyday proletarian life."

The approach of the Workplace Project Groups had some success. In October 1971, for example, a direct action of migrant workers during an Opel employees' meeting in Rüsselsheim was organized by Revolutionärer Kampf members. However, the approach did not spread as fast and as wide as the groups had hoped for and the original hopes were not met. The general difficulties of workplace organizing—surveillance and repression, the threat of layoffs, etc.—were one reason; the cultural barriers between the students and the "mass workers" another.

As the term "factory intervention" indicates, the impulse for class struggle in German factories did not, as in Italy, come from the workers themselves, but from student activists. The intention of the Workplace Project Groups was to bring their antiauthoritarian activism to the factories. They saw direct action and militancy as points of convergence between the antiauthoritarian revolt and "proletarian working-class culture." During their efforts, the differences to Italy become obvious:

> The contrast between the interests of the mass worker and of the organizations that act in his name is too big. . . . The mass worker has too often been sold as political bait and is extremely skeptical of all intellectual vanguards. . . . It seems that the notion of "workers' autonomy" is constructed in West Germany. It lacks a real basis, although pockets might exist. However, the road from passive to active forms of resistance is a long one, and the lack of identifying with one's

labor does not automatically mean that one identifies with left-wing radicalism, especially not one that comes from the outside. . . . The group Revolutionärer Kampf has realized this in self-critical evaluation. The wrong perceptions of the working class's radicalism and autonomy stemmed from the "Italian Illusion."

The development of capitalism in West Germany is very different to that of Italy, too. In Italy, the capitalist boom of the 1960s was based on "the exploitation of an apparently limitless workforce, on the rationalization of labor, on low wages, and on the proletarization of millions of rural workers, peasants, and the petty bourgeoisie after World War II" . . . i.e., mainly on the production of absolute surplus value. In West Germany, the production of relative surplus value was always central. Besides, the extensive accumulation strategy of capital ended in the late 1950s (Kukuck).

Even the strike movement of 1973 that peaked in the Ford walk-out in Cologne in late August was mainly carried by migrant workers. The Ford strike was passionately embraced by the radical left with its hitherto unknown forms of organization that contradicted the protocol of the DGB-SPD union apparatus. Yet no broad autonomous workers' movement developed. The Workplace Project Groups could not interfere decisively, and racist divisions between German and migrant workers could not be overcome, which contributed to the movement's defeat.

The Housing Struggles

In 1970, antiauthoritarian activists began to squat houses in Munich, Cologne, Frankfurt, Göttingen, Hamburg, and other German cities. The Workplace Project Groups embraced squatting as a means of political struggle mainly for two reasons: it allowed them to relate directly to "everyday proletarian life," and it opened up new possibilities of mobilization with the prospects in the factories being unsatisfactory.

Revolts in workers' hostels, tenants' strike movements, and housing struggles in general were seen as focal points of anticapitalist struggles in the spheres of reproduction. For the Workplace Project Groups, this confirmed that capital extended its control over all areas of social life and they popularized the term "housing factories." The Proletarische Front wrote in the May 1973 issue of *Wir wollen alles*:

"To squat means to destroy the capitalist plot for our neighborhoods. It means to refuse rent and the capitalist shoe box structure. It means to build communes and community centers. It means to recognize the social potential of each neighborhood. It means to overcome helplessness. In squatting and in rent strikes we can find the pivotal point of anticapitalist struggles outside of the factory."

The Workplace Project Groups hoped that the housing struggles would help them mobilize the proletarian need for collectivity against the capitalist division of labor. They aimed at uniting the interests of students and workers through everyday interaction and communication. They also hoped that the shared experience of militancy and state repression would bring people together. However, the reality of the housing struggles of the early 1970s was very different.

The housing struggles were most pronounced in Frankfurt and in Hamburg, cities governed by the Social Democrats. The squats drew cautious reactions from these city governments eager to appear reform-oriented. In Frankfurt, the SPD promised to fight land speculation. While the housing struggles in the city turned into a broad social movement, the struggle in Hamburg escalated after the eviction of the Ekhofstraße 39 squat. The eviction marked a defeat of the radical left in the city with far-reaching consequences. It also meant that squatting was no longer discussed as a mere praxis to live rent-free in empty buildings: for a few years, squatting would define radical discourse in West Germany. The development of the housing struggles proved that new forms of struggle were possible in the area of reproduction; forms that gained broad popular support at times, despite their illegality.

FRANKFURT

In the late 1960s, the leading banks of Frankfurt began an ambitious restructuring of the city into a bank and service industry metropolis. They intended to expand into the Westend neighborhood that was well connected to the city center. The Westend was the traditional home of Frankfurt's bourgeoisie. Land speculators bought a huge number of properties and rented them out to migrant families. This caused the departure of most of the traditional Westend residents and allowed the speculators to make huge profits off extortionate rents. Entire blocks became hopelessly overcrowded, while some properties were intentionally left vacant. It was practically impossible for students to rent collective apartments in the neighborhood.

It was during this period, from 1970 to 1974, that the Frankfurt squatters' movement developed. The driving force was antiauthoritarian students, who had already turned Frankfurt into an activist center during the student movement. The demise of the SDS chapter had spawned a strong Sponti scene. Many radicals also collaborated with migrant workers who had been part of the Lotta Continua group in Italy. In 1972–73 rent strikes, carried mainly by Turkish and Italian immigrants, were supported by Sponti squatters. However, the collaboration also caused conflict: limited political autonomy on the side of the rent strikers met with a "social worker and lawyer mentality" on the side of the Spontis. Furthermore, the relationship between the groups was based on pragmatism rather than political conviction.

The Frankfurt Sponti scene, with Revolutionärer Kampf as its most important group, dominated the public expression of the housing struggle until 1974. A variety of actions, demonstrations, and occupations were organized. Militancy was an important factor. In September 1971, the squatters received a lot of popular support after a failed eviction attempt. The movement managed to turn the momentum into further occupations and rent strikes. Frankfurt's SPD-led city council was forced to revoke its general order of immediate eviction.

When the rent strike movement of the migrant workers ended in the spring of 1973, the discussions within the radical left focused on the defense of the occupied houses and on the militant protection of mass demonstrations. When the Kettenhofweg squat was threatened with eviction, the Spontis opted for an aggressive political campaign. The police responded with measures of intimidation that were considered disproportionate even by the general public. Riots in Frankfurt's inner city were the consequence. Several eviction attempts could be repelled thanks to militant determination and widespread solidarity. In these conflicts, political information campaigns related to a form of mass militancy that was not detached from its goals but directly linked to them. The bourgeois press was deeply concerned: "In the hearts of our cities clusters of civil war are emerging. . . . Following the Frankfurt example, parallel governments might appear in other inner cities as well: yesterday university councils, today housing councils, tomorrow maybe the 'councils of occupied factories'" (*Frankfurter Neue Presse*, April 1973).

Eventually, the Kettenhofweg squat was evicted by brutal force. From then on, the militant protection of demonstrations became a main focus for Frankfurt's Spontis. Militancy and counterviolence were heatedly debated. The discussions were open and related directly to the broad squatters' movement, probably one reason why attempts at the criminalization of the militants failed at the time. However, the fixation on militant defense also overshadowed discussions on political perspectives. Partly, this was caused by the exhaustion of many activists due to the ongoing repression; partly, it was a consequence of Revolutionärer Kampf taking an increasingly dominant role. In early February 1974, another important Frankfurt squat, "The Block," was evicted in a surprise attack by 2,500 police. It was demolished immediately afterward. On February 23, a demonstration gathered ten thousand people and led to the biggest riots in Frankfurt during the 1970s. None of this changed the fact that the activists had suffered a blow at the hands of Frankfurt's city council. The squatters' movement in the city was practically at its end. The lack of political perspective was described by a Sponti: "Traditional power structures were reproduced in our own ranks, and people no longer knew what to do. When you keep people excluded from decision-making processes, you cannot be surprised if no one steps in once you have lost the track" (*Wildcat*, no. 40, 1986).

After the end of the housing struggle, the Sponti movement tried to maintain its political identity through a counterculture, specific campaigns, and militant actions. In the summer of 1974, there was a struggle around public transport fares; in September 1975, there was an attack on the Spanish General Consulate; and in May 1976, there was a militant demonstration of three thousand people after Ulrike Meinhof's death. All the while, there was clandestine organizing and the street militancy of small groups. The "small group concept" allowed for more effective confrontations with the police, but it also contributed to the fragmentation of a once united radical left.

Strongly linking revolutionary aspirations to street militancy backfires when street militancy is no longer practiced. The Spontis based their politics on individual needs. This entails a big danger: when difficult social conditions (weak revolutionary commitment, strong state repression, etc.) make collective resistance necessary, it might be nowhere to be found.

The Ekhofstraße 39 Squat in Hamburg

The story behind the Ekhofstraße squat begins with the plans of Bewobau, a subsidiary of the housing society Neue Heimat, to tear down numerous buildings in the inner city neighborhood of

Hohenfelde in order to build nineteen-storey apartment buildings with a total of 450 private luxury apartments. Preparations took years and included intentional displacements of long-term tenants. Students were encouraged to move in on short-term contracts. At the time of the Ekhofstraße 39 occupation, many houses in Hohenfelde were empty or rented out to students who were not considered potential long-term residents. All through this, the Neue Heimat collaborated with private speculators. The unscrupulous methods led to the foundation of a tenants' initiative, but the petitions, flyers, and open letters did not make much of an impression. So, on April 19, 1973, Ekhofstraße 39 was squatted:

> It was the first attempt by the Hamburg Spontis to put their ideas into practice. Revolutionary violence was a key issue, not least because of the expansion of the West German police apparatus and the increasing repression against the left, fuelled by the fight against the Red Army Faction. The example of the Kettenhofweg squat in Frankfurt provided an example for the possibility of mobilizing broad social groups around radical and uncompromising political struggles. The fact that an eventual confrontation with the repressive state apparatus had to be expected already influenced the preparations of the occupation and was expressed in the appearance of the activists who had brought helmets, balaclavas, and clubs (Grüttner).

In the beginning, there was a lot of neighborhood solidarity that ranged from the donation of furniture to solidarity banners suspended from other houses. The squatters reached out to the residents of the neighborhood, organized meetings where they discussed their ideas openly, and established a neighborhood bureau as well as a youth center. Especially for the neighborhood's youth, the squat became an important meeting place.

The popular support that the squatters received and their outspoken commitment to defend the house militantly made it impossible for the city council, the Bewobau, and the police to enforce an immediate eviction. Instead, they tried to isolate and criminalize the squatters. The propaganda part was handled by Hamburg's Springer press, which constantly referred to the squatters as "traveling radicals," "masked men," "political rockers," "terrorists," and "gangsters," fabricating stories about squatters attacking other neighborhood residents. The provocation part was handled by the police, which harassed the squatters on a daily basis, trying to restrict their options for broader political work. All residents, visitors, and sympathizers were stopped and controlled at the way to and from the squat. Many were taken to the station and forced to leave fingerprints. The squatters responded with organized militancy. However, a violent conflict with the police was not sustainable in the long run. Meanwhile, as the squatters were preoccupied with daily skirmishes with the police, political activism at the squat basically came to a complete halt. With the shift from the political to the militant plane, the solidarity of the neighborhood population also waned. Everyone was severely affected by the permanent presence of the police.

On the morning of May 23, 1973, the squat was sealed off by six hundred policemen and attacked by a SWAT team equipped with machine guns. More than seventy squatters were arrested, and thirty-three of them were charged with "membership in or support of a criminal organization" (§129), which later led to a number of convictions. It was the first time that the paragraph was used under such circumstances.

The events became a watershed for Hamburg's Spontis. As a consequence of the eviction, the Proletarische Front fell apart. The group members had supported the squat although it did not fit their theoretical convictions; according to them, the housing struggle had to be based in working-class neighborhoods and prepared by widespread public propaganda. When the Ekhofstraße 39 was occupied, many of the neighborhood residents had already left. There were few, if any, long-term political perspectives in Hohenfelde. Still, the Proletarische Front had fallen into one of the traps of militant politics: militancy became primarily an individual test of dedication and morality. Eventually, this tore the group apart.

In the wake of the eviction and the subsequent state repression, some of the Ekhofstraße squatters decided to go underground. Two of them, Karl-Heinz Dellwo and Bernhard Rößner, were part of the Red Army Faction commando that tried to force the release of the Stammheim RAF prisoners with an attack on the German embassy in Stockholm in Aoril 1975. The participation of former squatters in the action of an armed resistance group allowed the state to subsequently present squatting as a "way station for terrorists."

As a result of the "Ekhofstraße Trauma," Hamburg's Spontis were not able to organize bigger political initiatives for some years.

This only changed in 1976 with the fight against the construction of a nuclear power plant in Brokdorf.

The Sponti Movement at the Universities

The situation of university students had changed dramatically during the first half of the 1970s. Through technocratic "education reforms," the universities had become mass institutions. The number of students in West Berlin and West Germany more than tripled between 1960 and 1979, when they reached about one million. Politically, the situation was characterized by K-groups and left reformists. While the K-groups prioritized the "demands of class struggle" over "individual needs," many of the "left-wing scholars" who entered academia as a result of the 1968 revolt focused on exposing "bourgeois science," managing not only to turn their theses into academic careers but also to sell them as important contributions to the struggle.

The antitheoretical and antiacademic Spontis gained ground in university-based activism in the mid-1970s. With unconventional, funny, and imaginative actions they challenged the academic structures: in Münster, a pig was voted university president. In Ulm, a dog ran for the university senate. At the peak of their influence, in 1977–78, Spontis acted as student representatives at several universities.

The Sponti movement of the 1970s was characterized by a rich, and contradictory, array of protest, revolt, refusal, and escapist behavior. The political ideas were a blend of anti-institutional, direct-democratic, autonomous, and anarchist elements. The main target was bourgeois society.

At the end of the 1970s, after the disillusioning experiences with the "reform universities," the Spontis focused increasingly on alternative culture, neighborhood organizing, and antinuclear activism. The universities still provided a relatively free space that was used as a base to engage in other struggles.

The description of the Sponti movement would remain incomplete without mentioning its social-psychological dimensions: in abstract terms, it could be described as an attempt to create collective experiences hinting at the possibility of something different. In more concrete terms, Sponti groups had collective ambitions that were unreasonably high and that ended more than once in psychological drama rendering any political work impossible. An "ideology of affectedness" was linked to a "new inwardness," which regularly led to abandoning politics and retreating to collective houses, self-help groups, and drugs. The "antipolitical" credo of the Spontis could at times turn into mere privatism.

A Short History of the K-Groups

During the APO's demise, several SDS factions already displayed sympathies for Marxist-Leninist party models. Even groups from the antiauthoritarian milieu turned to dogmatism in their search for new political perspectives. Slogans like "Get Over Antiauthoritarianism" began circulating, and people started to speak of a "proletarian turn." The "antiauthoritarian craziness" of mostly middle-class students was replaced by a return to the "petty-bourgeois seriousness" of a Marxist-Leninist cadre. Individual ideas were abandoned and the party obeyed. Now, the party—usually referred to as the "leading party of the proletariat," no matter one's personal favorite—stood for "revolutionary identity," and no longer the individual. Among the many "K-groups" [*kommunistisch*] that formed, four became especially influential, some of them establishing a strong dominance in particular towns and regions: in West Berlin, the KPD-AO, founded in 1970; in Kiel and in the Ruhr Valley, the Kommunistische Partei Deutschlands–Marxisten-Leninisten (KPD-ML), founded in late 1968 by old KPD members; in Hamburg, the Kommunistische Bund (KB), founded in 1971; and in Frankfurt, Heidelberg, and Bremen the KBW, founded in 1973 by a number of study groups.

What all of the aforementioned organizations shared apart from the fixation on the revolutionary role of the factory proletariat was their "antirevisionist" stance against the DKP and the Soviet Union. The Maoist influence was strong, and the programs largely followed the policies of the People's Republic of China and Albania. Some organizations even criticized the Soviet Union for "social imperialism" and considered the country an even bigger enemy of revolutionary socialism than the United States. The KPD-ML and others also demanded a reunited "socialist German fatherland." Worst, however, was the K-groups' narrow-minded understanding of theory and practice and their organizational structures; authoritarian and dogmatic theory combined with dry economic doctrines reduced the universal horizon of Marxism-Leninism to a vulgar ideology of allotment gardens. Nonetheless, the groups' members were convinced of the "leading role of the party in the workers' struggle." This produced not only strictly hierarchical structures but also strict demands for obedience, discipline, and endurance. Party members were held to rigid standards of performance. Their everyday lives and social relationships were entirely regulated. Almost all private income was handed over to the party, "red weddings" were arranged, men had to keep their hair short, and people were expected to dedicate up to eighteen hours a day to "revolutionary party politics," while the Sponti scene was denounced as "elitist" and "petty-bourgeois."

In the mid-1970s, the K-groups formed the strongest extraparliamentary force of the left in various towns. At their peak, more than ten thousand people were organized in them. The KBW was the biggest organization with three thousand members, while the KB almost had one thousand in Hamburg alone. In 1977, the KBW journal *Kommunistische Volkszeitung* sold more than thirty thousand copies per week. The KB's *Arbeiterkampf* was not far behind with twenty-five thousand.

Some organizations showed a surprising level of militancy: in April 1973, members of the KPD-AO stormed and smashed Bonn's town hall in protest against the visit of the South Vietnamese prime minister. In 1975–76, the KBW organized massive tramway blockades against the rise in public transport fees. During the early stages of the nationwide antinuclear movement, the K-groups sent large contingents of well-equipped comrades who proved very effective in hands-on confrontations. It was not least their militancy that led to intensive discussions about prohibiting the K-groups, especially the KBW, in late 1977. A support rally, arranged by most of the prominent K-groups except the KB, drew about twenty thousand people to the Bonner Marktplatz; the square was covered in red flags.

The demise of the K-groups began soon after. The return to party concepts of the 1920s and an entirely anachronistic notion of the proletariat—modeled after the male factory worker—was a strategic joke under the late-capitalist conditions of West Germany. Furthermore, the K-groups had no answers to the pressing issues raised by the critique of patriarchy and the New Social Movements (antinuclear, environmentalist, and alternative). It became increasingly difficult to mobilize new members to submit themselves to an authoritarian party structure and to accept constant meddling in their private affairs.

After the demise of the K-groups, some cadres retreated from political work completely. Others joined the Green Party. In West Berlin's

Alternative Liste (AL), former KPD-AO members still caused irritation in the late 1980s with their calls for a "reunification of a German fatherland free from the superpowers." Other former K-group members, however, advanced to the highest ranks of the party after repenting for their "youthful revolutionary sins" and pledging allegiance to the constitutional state. Within Hamburg's KB there was a split. One wing collaborated with the Greens, the other continued as a decidedly communist organization.

By the late 1980s, there only existed a few remnants of the former K-groups in organizations like the Bund Westdeutscher Kommunisten (BWK), the Vereinigte Sozialistische Partei (VSP), and the Marxistisch-Leninistische Partei Deutschlands (MLPD). As a noticeable political force, they had disappeared. However, the Marxist-Leninist ideology of the 1970s still played a role in the development of the autonomous scene of the 1980s—not always in pleasant ways.

The Alternative Movement

The beginnings of the so-called alternative movement in West Germany and West Berlin were strongly rooted in a growing skepticism of workplace-focused politics. This became ever more pronounced toward the end of the 1970s. The alternative movement seemed to provide an escape route from state repression on the one hand and integration into the system on the other. It also appeared to offer the possibility to combine individual and collective emancipation—an ideal that the Spontis had already articulated during the time of the APO.

After the failure of the K-groups, people were looking for new forms of organizing. A movement pursuing a kind of "parallel culture" emerged, which tried to create a practical alternative to the dominant social order. It was strongest in the established centers of the radical left, particularly in Frankfurt and West Berlin.

In the beginning, many of the alternative projects saw themselves as everyday support structures for the general political struggle: left-wing bookstores, bars, cafés, print shops, etc. However, there was also a strong "utopian" element: all of these projects should provide tangible examples of a future socialist society established in the midst of capitalism. In this sense, the beginning of the alternative movement was strongly connected to the autonomous impulse of rejecting wage labor and resistance in everyday life.

The alternative movement developed under the "objective conditions" of economic crises. This led to a number of problems and contradictions. The rejection of alienated and repressive social structures often turned into individualistic and cynical self-marginalization. While the significance of small-scale production and distribution of goods in self-managed projects was ideologically exaggerated, the actual political relevance of the alternative movement became weaker and weaker. The term "alternative economy" soon functioned primarily as a label for a capitalist market niche. Ridiculously expensive organic apples or biodynamic carrots also fed into the emerging "health ideology," another capitalist bonus. In short, economic objectivity took priority over individual consciousness. By the end of the 1980s, most alternative projects were solidly integrated into the capitalist structure.

Autonomous circles have always formulated a strong critique of the alternative movement's illusions. They have stressed that the rejection of bourgeois society is not credible if its social foundation is not

SOLIDARITÄT ᴹᴵᵀ ᴅᴇᴿ ROTEN ARMEE FRAKTION !
FÜR DEN AUFBAU DER STADTGUERILLA !

challenged. The alternative movement took the rebellious elements from the factories and the streets and locked them into a ghetto. It also added ideologically veiled self-exploitation to the exploitation by capital. However, this critique—formulated in hindsight—remains "objectivist" itself and does not take the historical circumstances of the mid-1970s into account. Furthermore, it simplifies a complex phenomenon. There remain alternative projects that build on the principles of autonomy, self-organization, and the authentic expression of needs and interests. They understand themselves as laboratories of a true counterculture and a basis for the rejection of capitalist performance society. Karl-Heinz Roth said:

> The things that any earnest social revolutionary ultimately pursues can presently only be anticipated in their very basic forms: common property, egalitarian income, as little obligation to work and as much self-determination as possible, the transcending of gender contradictions, the dissolution of the nuclear family, decentralized self-management without bureaucracy and state structure, alternative technology, and the reconstruction of the natural environment. I am convinced that the first direct steps toward them are incredibly important because they are a beginning: a beginning of new hopes to prove that one day the gap between limited possibilities of self-realization and the general social goal can be bridged.

In some of the bigger cities, alternative projects allow people to organize most of their daily life in spaces of solidarity and relative freedom to this day. When the alternative movement was strongly criticized by West Berlin's squatters' movement in the early 1980s, it still provided the movement's economic basis. Furthermore, certain alternative projects continue to function as springboards for broader political struggles.

The Journal *Autonomie*

In October 1975, the journal *Autonomie* was launched with the revealing subtitle "Materials against Factory Society" [*Materialien gegen die Fabrikgesellschaft*]. The journal was a kind of a successor to *Wir wollen alles*, which had folded the same year. *Autonomie* served as the new theoretical forum for the groups that had once carried *Wir wollen alles* and

63

were now in a phase of political reorientation. *Autonomie* was published until 1985, with a longer break in 1978–79.

Until the end of 1978, the editorial collective was divided between Frankfurt and Hamburg. From 1979 on, the "New Series" [*Neue Folge*] was published only in Hamburg. The Frankfurt group left because two rather different, and increasingly opposed, strains had developed under the label *Autonomie*: the subjective-aesthetic Frankfurt strain and the analytical Hamburg strain.

The Hamburg group saw the term "autonomy" used by many as an excuse to turn away from truly revolutionary politics. They held on to a clearly Marxist and operaist orientation. The Frankfurt group, on the other hand, saw tendencies toward party politics developing in the Hamburg group, which violated their antiauthoritarian principles. Furthermore, the workplace struggles that the Hamburg group focused on were interpreted as reformist and the rising significance of the antinuclear struggles seemed to challenge a strong workplace focus.

In hindsight, the Hamburg group was certainly right in some of its assumptions: in the early 1980s, many former Spontis from Frankfurt ended up in the moderate "Realo" wing of the Green Party. The former *Autonomie* author Thomas Schmid even became a mentor for the "eco-libertarian" current on the right end of the Green Party: a tendency that tried to span an antisocialist arc from the Greens to the FDP and even members of the CDU.

Eventually, the Frankfurt group left the journal to the Hamburg collective which published *Autonomie* until 1985. The journal's main themes became the legacy of fascism in Germany, the revolutionary developments in Iran, the squatters' and the antinuclear movements, repression, the analysis of the Italian Autonomia project, the class analysis of imperialism in the industrialized nations, and the attempt to outline a "new anti-imperialism."

The journal's relationship to the emerging autonomous movement was ambivalent. On the one hand, the editors' focus was to provide "materials against factory society;" on the other hand, they had ambitions of more direct political intervention. However, their interventions either proved embarrassingly wrong (as in the case of Iran) or they were largely ignored by the autonomous movement.

The end of *Autonomie* in 1985 must not lead us to underestimate the journal's importance for the development of the Autonomen. It provided a historical bridge from the 1968 student revolt to the autonomous

SOZIALE REVOLUTION
GEGEN IMPERIALISTISCHE FLÜCHTLINGSPOLITIK

REVOLUTIONÄRE ZELLEN

scene of the 1980s. The political experience of some of the editors spanned the entire period. At a time of antitheoretical pragmatism, *Autonomie* tried to open spaces beyond the immediate everyday work of autonomous groups. In that way, the journal contributed to the political complexity of the movement.

The Urban Guerrilla and Other Armed Groups

There were close links between the Sponti milieu of the 1970s and the urban guerrilla groups Red Army Faction [Rote Armee Fraktion, RAF], 2nd of June Movement [Bewegung 2. Juni], and Revolutionary Cells/Red Zora [Revolutionäre Zellen/Rote Zora, RZ], but they were not without contradictions.

The emergence of both Spontis and armed groups was related to the demise of the extraparliamentary opposition as a mass movement, to the repression suffered by the APO, and to the partial integration of APO activists into the system. The armed groups raised the question of power very clearly: if you propagate revolution, you have to address organized mass violence and armed struggle. Personal integrity and personal identity were central aspects in the decision to join the armed groups. By doing so, one shut all backdoors for secret escape routes from political activism. Retreat and resignation were no longer options. However, the moral dimensions implied in picking up arms also made the choice of political struggle more limited. State repression added to this. The entire left was strongly affected by the ever-increasing repression of radical left politics in the wake of the armed groups' activities of the 1970s.

In the beginning, the RAF clearly tried to tie its actions to the militant grassroots politics of the APO. The communiqué after the Baader liberation was a prime example. Soon, however, the group stated that it was impossible to combine mass activism with guerrilla struggle. At around the time the K-groups emerged, the RAF also embraced authoritarian Marxist-Leninist cadre principles. This caused a rift between the RAF and the antiauthoritarian Spontis who rejected all notions of leadership.

With their anti-imperialist actions of May 1972—for example, the attack on the Heidelberg headquarters of the U.S. Army—the RAF tested their relationship to the K-groups, who they shared a common APO heritage with. However, most of the former APO comrades distanced themselves from the actions. The lack of solidarity and cowardice that the RAF faced led to a new orientation within the group. Now, the global anti-imperialist struggle became its focus. The RAF saw itself as a "First World" arm of the national liberation movements in the "Three Continents" (Africa, Asia, Latin America).

In 1972, practically the entire founding generation of the RAF was in prison. The prisons became new areas of agitation. RAF members fought particular hard against solitary confinement, which they referred to as "isolation torture" [*Isolationsfolter*]. Their central demand was shared detention [*Zusammenlegung*] for all RAF prisoners. To emphasize their commitment, RAF prisoners engaged in several hunger strikes.

From 1975 to 1977, new RAF members tried to force the release of their comrades with several actions. However, the "Free-the-Guerrilla Guerrilla" collapsed after the failed "1977 Offensive," which included actions against powerful individuals such as Siegfried Buback, Attorney General of Germany, Jürgen Ponto, chairman of the Dresdner Bank, and Hanns-Martin Schleyer, president of the Confederation of German Employers' Associations.

The 2nd of June Movement presented itself in 1972 as "an urban guerrilla organization of several autonomous groups." In contrast to the RAF, its politics mainly focused on the contradictions in the industrialized nations themselves:

> "2nd of June Movement" is a political term. It means to express the political resistance that emerged with the youth revolt of the 1960s in everyday life. The 2nd of June Movement is embodied by everyone who resists everyday capitalist terror and tries to find alternatives. This includes squatters and youths who create their own centers, prison and women's groups, self-managed kindergartens and alternative publication projects, the organization of rent strikes and abortions, and the internationalist solidarity committees with the peoples of Vietnam, Iran, Palestine, Angola, Western Sahara, and elsewhere. When the armed commandos were formed, they were an expression and a consequence of these activities, they came from them, they were nurtured by them, and they were dependent on them, even if some no longer want to acknowledge that. It was the attempt to express the latent revolutionary potential of the movement in exemplary actions and to push the movement forward by overcoming the feeling of helplessness, not least in relation to the power of

the police and the prisons (from an interview with Ronald Fritsch, Gerald Klöpper, Ralf Reinders, Fritz Teufel, 1978).

The 2nd of June Movement was based in West Berlin, where it organized a string of successful and popular actions, including a bank robbery where chocolate-coated marshmallow treats were handed out. The kidnapping of the prominent CDU member Peter Lorenz led to the release of a number of imprisoned comrades. However, by 1976, the group was strongly weakened due to the arrests of most of its members. Eventually, the 2nd of June Movement split into two factions: one followed the RAF's anti-imperialist course, while the other emphasized social-revolutionary activism.

The concept of the Revolutionary Cells and the women's guerrilla Rote Zora was similar to the "grassroots guerrilla" approach of the 2nd of June Movement. In 1981, some members reflected on the Revolutionary Cells' founding phase and their approach to militant struggle:

> In 1973, when the first Revolutionary Cell took responsibility for an action, we saw ourselves as the starting point of a mass movement that would engulf various sections of society. For us, there were many signs that justified this belief. The strike waves at factories like Hoesch, Mannesmann, John Deere, and Klöckner indicated new forms and goals of workplace struggles in Germany. In Cologne's Ford factory, the contours of a multinational and autonomously organized working class took shape. Many neighborhoods experienced unrest. The youth movement campaigned for self-determined youth centers, even in the smallest towns. The squatters' movement proved a readiness by people to take what they needed. Forms of resistance that were previously seen as purely personal were politicized, for example, shoplifting or riding public transport for free. The women's movement had rapidly turned into a strong social force, exemplified in the nationwide campaign against the "abortion paragraph" 218 in 1975. . . . The concept of armed struggle seemed a possibility to support these tendencies. The actions carried out by clandestine autonomous groups were meant to be the first steps toward an ongoing attack against the structures of domination. Our goal was to organize "counterpower" in small autonomous units that work, fight, intervene, and protect as elements of a mass movement. Once there are enough units, the guerrilla itself will become a mass movement (*Revolutionärer Zorn*, no. 1, May 1975).

It is interesting to note that the Revolutionary Cells never received the public attention that the RAF received, the institutionalized enemy of the West German state.

The German Autumn of 1977

Politically, West Germany experienced a number of significant political developments in 1977. There was the emergence of a massive militant antinuclear movement, reaching unprecedented levels with the occupation of the construction site at Grohnde in the spring. There was also a resurgence of RAF activism, two years after the occupation of the German embassy in Stockholm. In the spring, Siegfried Buback was killed, in the summer Jürgen Ponto. The kidnapping of Hanns Martin Schleyer, the "boss of bosses," on September 5 in Cologne, finally introduced the so-called German Autumn. The goal of the Schleyer action was to free RAF prisoners. The government immediately imposed a news embargo, willingly accepted by the media. The government also suspended all formal democratic procedures for forty-four days, handing powers to a "Crisis Management Team" [*Großer Krisenstab*] that violated the Constitution. The so-called Contact Ban [*Kontaktsperre*] was pushed through parliament with a complete disregard for regular protocol. It mandated complete isolation for all RAF prisoners: no newspapers, TV, or radio, and no visits by family or lawyers, let alone by anyone else. Basically, the prisoners were turned into state hostages. Their lawyers had been kept from visiting them even beforehand. A judge had ruled this practice illegal, but this was simply ignored.

Meanwhile, the antinuclear movement remained active: on September 24, it organized a mass demonstration against the construction of the fast breeder reactor in Kalkar. This raised state repression to a hitherto unknown level. Entire highways were shut down, at least 125,000 (!) IDs were checked, police helicopters stopped passenger trains, and buses were searched by police with machine guns. Most of the protesters never arrived at the planned manifestation, at least not on time. What became known as the "Kalkar Shock" within the movement led to partial demoralization.

With respect to the Schleyer kidnapping, the Crisis Management Team was trying to win time. The situation came to a dramatic head when an Arab commando hijacked a Lufthansa plane leaving Majorca on October 13. Taking random German tourists as hostages was meant to increase the pressure on the government and lead to the prisoners' release. The Crisis Management Team increased efforts to come to a military solution. Some figures, like CSU leader Franz-Josef Strauß and the federal prosecutor general Rebmann, even suggested liquidating the RAF prisoners. Eventually, the hijacking ended on October 17, when a commando of the GSG 9 [the counterterrorism unit of the German Federal Police] stormed the plane in Mogadishu [where it had landed earlier that day]. The next morning, the RAF prisoners Andreas Baader, Jan Carl Raspe, and Gudrun Ensslin were found dead in their cells. Irmgard Möller had life-threatening injuries. The prisoners had been under constant and exclusive surveillance by

GROHNDE, 1977

the state. It took only a few hours for the authorities to cite suicide as the cause of death, although the exact circumstances of the events have never been clarified. On the evening of October 18, Schleyer was found dead in a car in Strasbourg, France.

The "German Autumn" was a crucial and defining experience for the New Left. While some distanced themselves explicitly from the RAF and rallied around the state where it felt safest, most were left speechless and confused. The Spontis experienced enormous state repression. Entire neighborhoods were under siege and patrolled by police with machine guns, activists were searched at gunpoint, and meeting places were raided.

The German Autumn hit the nondogmatic left in a phase of re-orientation. The factory interventions and squatting struggles had been lost, while the antinuclear movement promised new possibilities, even if there had not been any great victories so far. In this context, both the Kalkar Shock and the RAF Offensive brought new challenges. The rift between many nondogmatic radicals and the RAF widened, and the Spontis were increasingly isolated from the left-liberal and academic 1968 activists who had made their peace with the state. For many, the German Autumn was a traumatic experience.

A Journey to TUNIX

In January 1978, a TUNIX [as in: *tu nichts*, "don't do anything"] meeting was organized in West Berlin. The organizers were mainly Spontis protesting the "Model Germany" [*Modell Deutschland*], which stood for harsh state repression in the wake of The German Autumn. The rise of a possible new fascism was discussed, and a Russell Tribunal on the human rights situation in West Germany was prepared. Spontis published the following call:

> We are fed up with this country! The winter is too sad, the spring too contaminated, and the summer too suffocating. The smell from the offices, the reactors, the factories, and the highways is unbearable. The muzzles no longer taste good and neither do the plastic-wrapped sausages. The beer is as flat as bourgeois morals. We no longer want to do the same work and make the same faces day in and day out. We have been ordered around long enough. We have had our thoughts, our ideas, our apartments, and our IDs controlled. We have had our faces smashed in. From now on, we refuse

> to be arrested, insulted, and turned into robots. We are leaving for the beaches of Tunix!

At the time of the meeting, the Sponti scene experienced developments that can roughly be summarized by three catchphrases: "Mescalero Urban Indians," "Crisis of the Left," and "Two Cultures."

By the mid-1970s, the Sponti left had become very popular among different grassroots initiatives. The popularity increased with the demise of the K-groups. Spontis were active as student representatives in a number of universities. In this context, the "Urban Indian" movement developed, influenced by its Italian counterpart.

The Urban Indians raised most attention with an obituary for Siegfried Buback that was published by the Göttingen comrade "Mescalero" in the spring of 1977. The author expressed "secret joy" about Buback's assassination, even if the text put this into perspective: "Our goal, namely to create a society without terror and violence (aggression and militancy is something different), a society without forced labor (hard work is something different), and a society without courts and prisons (rules and regulations, or better: suggestions, are something different), does not justify all means, only some. Our way to socialism (for me: anarchy) cannot be paved with corpses."

Even though the text included a clear critique of the RAF it triggered a massive wave of state repression against the nondogmatic left in the entire country. In Göttingen, houses and apartments were searched, and more than one hundred preliminary proceedings were initiated against publishers that had reprinted the text, which had originally appeared in the paper of Göttingen's student council. When a number of university professors signed a reprint of the text, they were disciplined. In Lower Saxony, the professors were forced to declare their "loyalty to the state." Peter Brückner refused and was suspended from his job.

While the radical left overcame many internal conflicts to pull together amid the wave of repression, it became divided along the question of violence. This provided the background for the TUNIX meeting. It reflected resignation and a wish to escape as much as a spirit of anarchist revolt. In the end, the meeting did help the Spontis regain self-confidence after the German Autumn. The organizing collective, which went by the name of Quinn the Eskimo, Frankie Lee, and Judas Priest, stated:

The weakness of the left was and is grounded in its inability to disclose the subtle mechanisms of domination and to counter them with subversive strategies. Dissatisfaction was an important element in the "mass success" of TUNIX. But it is not only a dissatisfaction with the state of West Germany (which is widespread among the population, at least under the surface), but also with the strategies of change that are being offered. There was a need to come together with others who felt the same.

Personally, we were also dissatisfied with the behavior of many of us. We saw it as a denial of our identity to distance ourselves from comrades' actions or to make strategic concessions to the overall political climate. In this sense, there was probably a moment of defiance in our calling for TUNIX; a sense of "right now we have to be particularly radical." Our identity is that of the radical left. If we deny this, only cynicism remains.

This sentiment was also expressed at the final march of the meeting. Here is a description from the bourgeois *Tagesspiegel* (January 29, 1978):

For the first time in years, a demonstration in Berlin turned violent. When a crowd of about five thousand people gathered to end the three-day TUNIX meeting at the Institute of Technology, paint bombs were thrown at the police outside the women's prison in Lehrter Straße and cobblestones outside the court house in Moabit's Turmstraße. The protesters included Spontis, Urban Indians, and other nonorganized leftists. They came from Berlin, West Germany, and Western Europe. . . . Swastikas and SS runes were painted on police vehicles. . . . The American House in Hardenbergstraße was bombarded with rocks. . . . A huge German flag saying "Modell Deutschland" was pulled through the streets by a sound truck. At the corner of Kurfürstendamm and Joachimstaler Straße, the flag was burned with police and passers-by watching. . . . Anarchists carried banners saying, "Stammheim Is Everywhere," "Away with the Dirt!" and "Gross!" Graffiti was painted on houses along the marching route, for example, "Free the Agit Printers" [Agit was a radical printers' collective] and "Anarchy Is Possible." Outside several prisons, the protesters chanted, "Free the Prisoners!"

The TUNIX organizers had managed to mobilize fifteen to twenty thousand people within a month. This proved that radical communication and information channels were still intact. TUNIX was the peak of the German Sponti movement. While the Spontis had proven themselves capable of organizing a mass event shortly after the German Autumn, the aftermath of the meeting saw the reality of "Two Cultures" take shape.

The term "Two Cultures" came from Italy where it had emerged in the conflict between the Autonomia movement and the Communist Party. In West Germany, it was first used as a propaganda term by SPD members who sketched new strategies of integrating the radical left. The intention was to incorporate, and thereby pacify, the resistant and autonomous impulses of the emerging alternative movement into official "political discourse." Alternative culture should become a "social laboratory," a "testing ground" for majority culture. Social democracy would then make the most innovative impulses profitable for modern bourgeois society. Unfortunately, the idea of "Two Cultures" was also embraced emphatically by parts of the Sponti scene that seemed flattered by this recognition from high above. The term also strengthened the illusion that one could leave behind "capitalist majority culture" by indulging in "alternative counterculture."

The years 1978–80 saw an unprecedented number of alternative economic projects emerging in West Berlin and West Germany; a tendency that had developed after the housing struggles in Frankfurt had become a nationwide trend. West Berlin turned into the secret capital of the alternative movement. A 1979 survey claims that about a hundred thousand people in the city counted themselves, at least in a wider sense, among the alternative scene.

However, the process of integrating the alternative scene into the system was far from smooth. Especially in West Berlin, the alternative movement also provided a strong basis for the radical squatters' movement that emerged in 1979–80. In 1981, after a wave of occupations, a TUWAT [*tu was*, "do something"] congress was organized. Among other things, attempts were made to relate the theories of the Italian Autonomia movement to the local housing struggles. This was but one example for the continuity of radical history.

II. THE MAKING OF THE AUTONOMEN IN THE 1980S

Fᴿᴏᴍ 1980 ᴛᴏ 1983, ᴛʜᴇʀᴇ ᴡᴀs ᴀɴ unexpected rise of New Social Movements in West Berlin and West Germany. Partly, these movements emerged from the alternative movement—at least in the towns and regions where it still had countercultural integrity. They also developed from certain single-issue campaigns (antinuclear, squatting, Startbahn-West, peace) that had widened their political perspective. Finally, they were triggered by the European social revolts of 1980–81, with the events of Zurich and Amsterdam being of particular influence. Bourgeois sociologists and journalists regularly spoke of "youth revolts," which was misleading. Most of the protagonists did not revolt because of their "youth" but because of deep social and political dissatisfaction. The term "youth revolt" also neglected the political history of the events. Without years of political organizing, the so-called youth revolt would have expressed itself in sporadic flares of misguided youthful militancy rather than in actions against nuclear power plants and airports and in protests against housing policies and so on. Many older comrades reacted to the revolt with surprise, since they had assumed they would no longer see street militancy of that kind after the German Autumn.

Within the New Social Movements, an autonomous wing formed: militant and mainly carried by young activists. They were strongly influenced by the "No Future" attitude of the time, confronted bourgeois norms of control and domination, and turned their own needs into a central political issue. So-called general assemblies [*Vollversammlungen*] replaced the university teach-ins of the 1960s and 1970s as the central form of communication. The general assemblies created a space outside the bourgeois public to discuss political goals and strategies. This chapter will describe the history of the Autonomen during the first half of the 1980s, especially in connection to the New Social Movements.

The New Social Movements attempted to provide solutions to the social and political conflicts that had beset the Western capitalist states since the mid-1970s. In the late 1970s, left-liberal academics and students used the term to suggest a continuity of the 1968 student revolt. However, the New Social Movements were strongly influenced by middle-class perspectives. In the academic evaluation of the New Social Movements, the Green Party has often been interpreted as a successful political manifestation of grassroots currents, and the "modernist" impulse of the New Social Movements and their contribution to a "change of values" has been stressed. In fact, some representatives of the nuclear mafia were grateful for the antinuclear movement since it helped prevent or delay projects that were not profitable. Furthermore, even the directors of power plants like to live healthy, shop in muesli stores, and eat wholesome biodynamic food. In a sense, the *Weltgeist* of New Social Movement research managed to unite formerly opposed political ideas in Uncle Habermas's new social democratic "Project of Modernity." In the green-alternative dimmer, terms like "class struggle" or "imperialism" appeared antiquated and irrelevant. Important were "qualitative needs," "participation," and "comanagement." Scholars even managed to convince many folks that the militant antinuclear struggles of Brokdorf and Grohnde, with their strong anticapitalist and antiauthoritarian implications, had been caused by nothing but a "failure of communication" and by a "lack of participation" in the planning of an energy supply system that, in the end, was very effective and beneficial to everyone. Whatever. It is not our problem if certain academics see the Autonomen as nothing but a "challenge" to the alternative movement that arose from "new poverty." This only proves that some scholars know very little about the stuff they are supposed to be experts in. But enough with the polemics.

The New Social Movements are strongly related to Fordism, the capitalist structure that defined most Western countries after World War II. Fordism is characterized by alienating mass production (epitomized by the assembly lines of the automobile factories), mass consumption, and a political as well as a legal regulation of class conflicts. The institutionalization of class antagonisms also means that negotiations usually happen outside of the sphere of production, especially in West Germany. In this context, the term "New Social Movements" tries to explain the composition, potential, and significance of grassroots movements that emerged unexpectedly at a time when there was practically no open class struggle in the country. The antinuclear movement, for example, formed in the sphere of reproduction and had a very complex class structure. For quite some time, it was opposed by the official workers' movement, especially in the nuclear and energy industries, where the reformist unions of the DGB mobilized skilled workers in decidedly pronuclear campaigns.

While many activists had middle-class background, they were very open to egalitarian structures and anticapitalist goals. It is true that certain lobby groups (for example, big farmers with relation to the antinuclear movement) have exploited the openness of the New Social Movements for their own interests. After all, many folks do not care who supports them in a struggle they deem important (for example, against a nuclear power plant in their town) as long as they get support. This, however, does in no way diminish the political significance of these movements. It only shows how challenging it can be to overcome certain cultural barriers within social movements. Comrades from the Red Aid West Berlin made a very illuminating statement in 1973 after K-groups had critiqued the emergence of *Bürgerinitiativen* (BI), "citizens' initiatives":

> Both the rigid antirevisionism and the exclusive concentration on proletarian organization has led to a left that has lost touch with reality. The left has completely ignored the conflicts in the area of reproduction. The emergence of the BIs has made this evident. The problem might have been more than disinterest, however. The liquidation of the antiauthoritarian movements meant that two important aspects

of political praxis were lost: grassroots activism in neighborhoods and workplaces (often ridiculed as "dilettantism")
and direct action (often derided as "spontaneism"). Neither
aspect was considered of use for the organization of the
working class; instead, they were deemed expressions of petty-bourgeois culture. The rigid use of class identity delegitimized the antiauthoritarian movements and reduced their
protagonists to representatives of their social origins. This
happened even though antiauthoritarian movements had, in
fact, overcome class differences through common mass action. . . . According to the left's critique of the BIs, eloquent
and competitive middle-class activists always took control.
However, such a strict definition of class denies political experience and merely reproduces sociological facts. What is
important is not the mere fact that members of different
classes unite in BIs. What is important is how this affects
class identity, whether it helps overcome class differences,
and how the mixture of class backgrounds can be made politically productive. It would be the task of a current class
analysis to examine whether the common struggle for specific interests challenges class differences (*Kursbuch*, no. 31).

These lines reveal how misleading the term "middle class" can
be. This is a problem that also affects radical left and autonomous circles. Especially when used in simplified and derogatory ways, the term
"middle class" can easily conceal class realities in the industrialized
nations. The development of capitalism in West Germany has brought
increased wealth for large parts of the lower classes, even if the overall
distribution of wealth remains unjust. In the 1950s, it became possible
for many workers to participate in the Economic Miracle to a degree
that made them integral parts of consumer society. This contributed
strongly to discrediting oppositional and communist forces. German
capitalism has made class identities more fluid while maintaining the
bourgeois structure of domination. This contributes strongly to the
system's stability. However, the same development has also created
new possibilities for action: "Fordism equips an ever-growing number
of people with the time and the skills that are necessary for continuous noninstitutional action. . . . In addition, the dissolving of traditional forms of organization in the church or in traditional workers'
organizations as well as the increase of cultural forms of expression
expands the range of individual action" (Hirsch/Roth). The strong
presence of students and academics—that is, "middle-class" folks—in
the radical left and autonomous movements is but a consequence of
these developments.

Not least due to the challenges they posed for class identity, the New Social Movements have shaken up, questioned, and challenged many aspects of the existing social order and have hence opened spaces in which the autonomous movement could emerge. Although the Autonomen go far beyond the limits of the New Social Movements, both in terms of political demands and political praxis, they are strongly linked to them. The term "New Social Movement" is also more appropriate than the term "class struggle" to describe the phenomenon of the autonomous movement. References to class were never missing ("Housing Struggles Are Class Struggles!"), but they often seemed far-fetched and were never widely used.

THE ANTINUCLEAR MOVEMENT: 1975-81

T HE WEST GERMAN ANTINUCLEAR MOVEMENT was a response to the new energy policies that followed the so-called Oil Crisis of 1973. Nuclear power was hailed as the new solution to the energy crisis, and nuclear power plants were planned in rural regions as cheap and productive pillars of Germany's power supply. Big corporations planned massive industrialization programs, including steel plants and pharmaceutical factories. A strong focus was put on the development of economically weak regions like the Unterelbe and the Oberrhein. Facing the horror scenario of "new Ruhr Valleys," the first broad popular protest movement formed in the border triangle of France, Germany, and Switzerland. The construction of several nuclear power plants could be prevented through occupations of the construction sites—for example, in Whyl in Baden-Württemberg.

The resistance in Whyl reached its peak with the storming and the occupation of the construction site in February 1975, when thirty thousand people participated in a protest march. The dimensions of the resistance caught the state completely off guard. Police units deployed at the site were recalled. Panic spread among the authorities. The minister president of Baden-Württemberg, Hans Filbinger, an old Nazi, remarked: "If this example is followed by others, the whole country will become ungovernable!" The site remained occupied until a decision by the constitutional court suspended the construction indefinitely and the authorities promised amnesty for all protesters.

The antinuclear conflicts in the Oberrhein region were largely carried by conservative, at times even reactionary, environmentalists and by local farmers and vintners. A blend of ecologist, traditionalist, and regionalist arguments dominated the debate. However, support also came from left-wing scholars in Freiburg and the Freiburg KBW chapter, and some actions already had clearly anticapitalist implications. For example, the collaboration between state authorities and energy corporations was widely publicized. Certain contradictions within the movement were overcome by common learning experiences, which changed the everyday life of many activists. Overall, the protests sent a signal that successful extrainstitutional resistance was still possible. For the radical left, this was of great importance after the defeat in the housing struggles and amid ever-increasing state repression.

Brokdorf

The radical left began to be a major factor in the antinuclear struggle when a protest movement emerged against the planned construction of a nuclear power plant in Brokdorf in the Unterelbe region, another area under development, not too far from Hamburg. A number of villages were destroyed and its inhabitants "relocated," as the technocrats call it; in more straightforward terms, thousands of people were forcibly displaced to make space for the construction of pharmaceutical factories and nuclear power plants. When the plans for yet another nuclear power plant in the area of Brokdorf-Wewelsfleht were made public, the Bürgerinitiative Unterelbe Umweltschutz (BUU) was founded. Similar initiatives followed, reaching all the way to Hamburg.

On October 30, 1976, there was a first demonstration of eight thousand people. A part of the planned construction site was occupied. After dark, the occupiers were brutally dispersed by the police. On November 14, there was a second demonstration in Brokdorf. This time, forty thousand people attended. For the first time in West German history, units of the Federal Border Guard were deployed at a protest. This was possible because of the emergency laws adopted in 1968. The protesters still managed to dismantle long stretches of the security fence. The police eventually attacked and broke up the demonstration with gas grenades shot from helicopters.

However, the tactics of intimidation did not work. The antinuclear movement grew rapidly after the police intervention and BIs against the nuclear program emerged all over the country. Several construction sites were stormed and protesters engaged in a number of clashes with the police. The movement was able to merge the resistance of the local population with concepts of militant mass struggle.

Political and Social Composition of the
Antinuclear Movement in the 1970s

A first split in the antinuclear movement occurred during the preparations for the third Brokdorf demonstration. A legal wing, consisting of SPD and DKP members as well as most BIs, found itself opposed to a militant wing, consisting of more radical BIs, K-groups, Spontis, and nonorganized activists. Another split occurred in Hamburg, where the BUU chapter got divided into a wing associated with the KB and an independent wing. Furthermore, the "nonviolent" sections of the movement started to focus on a particular struggle in the spring of 1977, namely the resistance against the planned nuclear waste dump in Gorleben. Urban activists, celebrities, and the local bourgeoisie had formed the Bürgerinitiative Lüchow-Dannenberg, which pursued a strictly nonviolent concept of resistance and excluded all other forms. Further divisions were caused by the many "Green," "Colorful," and "Alternative" lists that formed in the context of the antinuclear movement and ran for local and regional councils as precursors of the Green Party. These lists united a variety of folks: socially secure middle-class activists on the margins of the BIs, academics and artists escaping the cities, teachers, farmers, freelance scholars, and even "socially conscious" bureaucrats. In rural regions, the lists mainly consisted of conservatives and reactionaries, while in urban areas they often gathered disillusioned SPD, FDP, and K-group members.

Nonorganized activists—who would later form the bulk of the Autonomen—were an important element of the militant wing and emerged as a strong political force in their own right. They were central for the disclosure of "neutral" and "objective" science working in the interest of the state. For the first time in West Germany, activists of the radical left formed a considerable part of a broad citizens' movement.

The BIs and environmental initiatives were often seen as the "extraparliamentary opposition of the average citizen." Their members mostly had middle-class backgrounds. This caused confusion among the most orthodox sections of the left, especially Marxist-Leninist groups that still focused on factory workers as the core element of

GORLEBEN

WENN SIE DICH FRAGEN, WIE KONNTE DAS GESCHEHEN
KANNST DU DANN SAGEN, DU HAST ES NICHT GEWUSST?

social liberation. Hamburg's KB, for example, ridiculed, defamed, and sometimes even interfered with the "petty-bourgeois" antinuclear movement of Brokdorf.

The rapid development and relative success of the antinuclear movement in 1976–77 did not only come as a surprise to the state but also to wide parts of the radical left. It expressed the hope of many that at least partial victories over the state and corporate lobbies were possible. In this sense, the antinuclear movement was far more than a single-issue affair. It was a focal point for challenging the dominant social conditions and attracted a wide variety of oppositional forces. The praxis of the nonorganized activists was reminiscent of the best moments of the 1968 student revolt. At times, they had a huge influence on the direction that the antinuclear struggles of 1976–77 were taking.

The core principle of the nonorganized activists was "practical resistance," by which they meant that each individual could partake in the struggle self-determinedly. For them it was crucial that the protest of the BIs was not purely rhetorical, but that practical steps were taken to meet the demands, even if this required breaking bourgeois notions of morality or the legal framework of the constitutional state. This approach was particularly popular since the decentralized character of the antinuclear movement provided a certain level of protection against state repression. It was in this context that the term "Autonome" began to signify a particular strain of activists. Autonome stressed the importance of immediate and self-responsible behavior. Public actions were announced in advance and illegal actions explained afterward. Personal identity was of little relevance and usually hidden. Elections were rejected as useless because people could not be motivated to do the right thing (to act practically and independently) by propagating something that was wrong (to vote).

In September 1978, Hamburg's Arbeitskreis Politische Ökonomie described the organizational structure of the antinuclear movement thus:

> It is not enough to have the "right" analysis of society and to disclose the laws it abides to. Instead, we need self-determined social structures. For now, these structures might only be possible as structures of resistance, but they can lead to actual change once people realize that they can take matters into their own hands and threaten the dominant economic and political structures. It is mandatory to develop trust in one's own abilities. Social change is not created by

replacing some individuals in power with others, even if they profess socialist or communist ideals. Social change comes from people being actively involved in the political decisions that affect them. The crucial principles are autonomy, equal rights, and direct action. It is therefore necessary to build independent structures of communication and coordination. A revolutionary movement is not just a result of "objective conditions"; it is the result of the structures we are able to build (*Bilanz und Perspektiven*).

1978–80: Can You Close Drill Holes with Fences?

In 1980, the autonomous groups within the antinuclear movement propagated the slogan "Let's Put the Fence of Brokdorf into the Drill Holes of Gorleben!" At the same time, there was an occupation of the drilling site in Gorleben in the spring of 1980 and the "Village 1004" as well as the "Free Republic of Wendland" were proclaimed—all under the premises of dogmatic nonviolence. [Wendland is a common name for the region containing Gorleben.] This caused severe conflict. While nonviolent activists wanted the Village 1004 to be a peaceful alternative idyll, the Autonomen wanted it to be the base of direct action against the nuclear mafia. Eventually, the Autonomen lost and left.

In early July 1980, the Free Republic of Wendland was destroyed in a military-style raid by ten thousand cops. Although the roughly two thousand occupiers did not actively resist the eviction, they were tortured and some severely injured. The spokespeople of the nonviolent activists saw this as a "big moral victory." Autonome commented: "The state not only manages to hurt people with batons and machine guns. It also manages to infiltrate their heads, thoughts, feelings, and desires" (*Anti-AKW-Telegramm*).

The Brokdorf Resistance, 1980–81

Shortly after the parliamentary elections of October 1980, the SPD-led West German government confirmed, together with the CDU-led government of Schleswig-Holstein, that the construction of the nuclear power plant in Brokdorf would continue. BIs from Northern Germany organized a demonstration at the construction site with eight thousand people. The fence surrounding the site was

BROKDORF, 1977

attacked and people managed to set fire to a water cannon. The successful demonstration rekindled broad resistance against the Brokdorf plant. In Hamburg, the offices of the Hamburgische Electricitäts-Werke (HEW) and the houses of HEW directors were attacked with petrol bombs. Meanwhile, the BIs prepared for a demonstration at the extraordinary party convention of Hamburg's SPD in Brokdorf in early February 1981. This led to a political split within the movement. While the Jusos and the DKP wanted to use the demonstration to strengthen their position in negotiations with the SPD leadership, the Autonomen wanted to establish themselves as a self-determined and independent political force. When the DKP and the Jusos seemed unable to convince the movement of their approach, they began to denounce autonomous activists. This, however, only weakened their position within the movement further. Eventually a demonstration was organized in Hamburg by Autonomen, the KB, and some BIs. It was prohibited by the Hamburg Senate. Undeterred, ten thousand people participated in a march on February 2. On the same day, a demonstration organized by the Jusos attracted about two thousand people.

Along the route of the big demonstration, the windows of banks, luxury hotels, insurance companies, and sex shops were smashed, and a camera store looted. There were heavy clashes with the police when the protesters tried to enter the city center. Autonome from Hamburg declared in a speech: "We have to engage in resistance that is not confined to the weekend or any particular place. The resistance has to encompass our entire life. Our strength does not come from technological superiority over the police and other state apparatuses, and neither from strict organization or from clever bargaining with politicians. It comes from our own political and strategic ideas, our own structures of communication, and our own ways of life. . . . If the law threatens our life, then we have every right to break the law" (*Anti-AKW-Telegramm*).

Some weeks later, the BIs mobilized for an even bigger demonstration. The media responded with the usual slander. On February 22, *Bild* ran the headline, "Brokdorf: Bombs, Fires, Kidnappings?" All demonstrations in the area of the construction site were banned, which basically meant a suspension of civil law. On February 28, the anti-nuclear movement managed to channel one hundred thousand people past the police barriers. This was a huge logistic success. Autonomous groups had been centrally involved in the planning. They had also prepared a Plan B, in case the police barriers proved impenetrable: return to Hamburg for "effective actions." Aware of this, the police tried

"TURN THE CONSTRUCTION SITE BACK INTO MEADOWS!"

Brokdorf 81:

8 Jahre Widerstand — Der Kampf geht weiter!

28.2.81
Großdemo am Bauplatz

In Brokdorf haben w
1976/77 auf mehreren Dem
am Bauzaun gezeigt, daß w
entschlossen sind, auch w
tant gegen den Bau vo
AKW's zu kämpfen. Durch u
seren Widerstand und de
mehrjährigen Kampf der ö
lichen Bevölkerung wur
Ende 76 ein Baustopp r
reicht. Die Atommafia h
immer wieder versucht, u
seren gemeinsamen Kam
zu zerstören, uns in gew
freie und militante AK
Gegner zu spalten, und dam
unserem entschlossenen
derstand die Spitze abzub
chen.

Nachdem vor einem Jahr d
Baustopp aufgehoben w
de, hat am 6.2.81 der Weit
bau begonnen. Die Pappn
sen von der Bundesreg
rung und der schleswi
holsteinischen CDU Lande
regierung wollen damit e
Weichen für die weite
Durchsetzbarkeit des Ato
programms stellen.

Doch wir werden nicht tate
los zusehen! euch
Leute, bereitet schon jetzt
Gruppen auf die Demo vor.
wird bestimmt kein Spazie
gang werden.

Wir wissen, daß das AK
Brokdorf und das Atompro
gramm nicht durch eine e
zelne Demo verhindert we
den kann, wir müssen u
deshalb auf einen langfris
gen und vielseitigen Wid
stand einstellen.

KEIN AKW IN BROKDORF UN
AUCH NICHT ANDERSWO!!!
Informiert Euch bei unsere
Kontakttelefon: Freunde d
Erde, 692 87 73 ab Monta
den 16.2.81 täglich von 16-
Uhr.

Spendenkonto: Sonderkon
Werner Kronawitter, Po
scheckamt Berlin Wer
Konto-Nr.: 34 75 15 -107, 10
Berlin 21

to wear the protesters out by delaying the start of the demonstration and making access to the departure point difficult and tiresome. In addition, they employed the usual means of repression. Protesters who left the demonstration were chased by helicopters, while SEK units had gathered from around the country, hunted down protesters, and severely injured several of them. The activists were rather reserved. Militancy was mainly used to protect oneself from police violence. Unfortunately, the police tactics seemed to pay off. Many protesters appeared tired and there were no significant attacks on the construction site. Still, for the first time after the Kalkar Shock the antinuclear movement had been able to organize a big common demonstration. But whatever "moral victory" might have been won that day, it was not enough to stop the resumption of the plant's destruction only two days later. As a consequence, there was a series of direct action and sabotage against construction firms in the region—the property damage was significant. However, these actions could not halt the construction process either and they did not trigger militant mass resistance.

The victory of the powerful in Brokdorf—specifically, a victory of the Northern German SPD—boosted the nuclear mafia, which rapidly started the construction of several more nuclear power plants. It took almost two years until the antinuclear movement was able to mobilize again nationwide for a big demonstration.

The political strength of the autonomous groups of Northern Germany, however, was far from crushed by the Brokdorf defeat. The Autonomen simply shifted their focus. On May 6, 1980, many autonomous groups were involved in militant protests against a parade of the German Army. The Autonomen made it increasingly clear that resistance must not limit itself to particular sites and issues, but had to entail "housing struggles, antiwar struggles, . . . struggles against prison torture, [struggles against everything] that destroys our resources and our environment and that leads to alienated living and working conditions" (*Brokdorf 28.2.81: Berichte Bilanz und Perspektiven*).

In 1981–82, many autonomous activists were engaged in protests against the criminalization of antinuclear activists in the so-called Brokdorf trials. At one point during the last Brokdorf demonstration, a SEK officer had been disarmed and prevented from further action. Based on a sensationalist press photo, the Ministry of the Interior of Schlewig-Holstein initiated a nationwide manhunt for "attempted murder." The intention was to both discredit and intimidate the antinuclear movement. The Autonomen countered with their own

BROKDORF PROZESSE

Michael Ouffke seit 7 Mon. im Knast.

min. 13 Prozesse werden vorbereitet.

min. 15 Ermittlungs-verfahren laufen.

Ermittlungen gegen 7 BUU Mitglieder wegen Verdacht auf Bildung einer terroristischen Vereinigung (§§ 129, 129ª)

Termine + Infos: Ökoladen Turner str. 9 HH6 Tel. 432364
Spenden: Stichwort Brokdorf Nr. 1118413
BLZ 20030000 Vereins-und Westbank

FREIHEIT FÜR ALLE AKW-GEGNER

information campaign, which eventually led to the murder accusation being dropped. In their solidarity work, the Autonomen declared militant resistance to the construction of nuclear power plants and attacks on cops legitimate. This spirited tactic could not prevent the drastic sentences against Markus and Michael, but it led to widespread public outcry over them.

A Short Summary

The antinuclear movement in West Germany was successful in ways that no one could have predicted. It managed to bring the energy policies of the third most powerful country on the planet to a temporary halt. It also sent a strong message to the "Model Germany" propagated by the SPD under Chancellor Helmut Schmidt. The Model Germany was based on the combination of export-oriented world market capital and a strong unionized skilled workers' class. The antinuclear struggles of the 1970s contributed significantly to the model losing much of its appeal.

In hindsight, the Brokdorf struggles constituted one of the cradles of the West German autonomous movement. At a time when the K-groups disbanded and the Green Party was founded, the Autonomen managed to form as an independent political faction.

"IN THE CASE OF EVICTIONS IN KREUZBERG 36 — FIGHT, FRIENDS!"

THE SQUATTERS' MOVEMENT
IN WEST BERLIN:
1980–83

IN 1980–81, A NEW SQUATTING WAVE SWEPT over the country. Its center was West Berlin. Up to 160 buildings were occupied at a time. The squatters' movement in Berlin built on years of neighborhood and tenants' initiatives against housing speculation and gentrification. The *Instandbesetzungen* [a German wordplay that combines occupation, *Besetzung*, and restoration, *Instandsetzung*] started in 1979 by the Bürgerinitiative SO 36 ["SO 36" stands for the eastern and economically weakest part of the district, also referred to as "Kreuzberg 36"] and different tenants' organizations. On December 12, 1980, an attempt by the police to prevent an occupation led to the so-called 12/12 riot, which gave the movement an enormous boost. For the first time, many nonsquatters took part in the rioting and the harsh repression by the police led to broad solidarity with the squatters' movement. Support committees demanded the immediate release of all imprisoned activists, issuing the warning that otherwise "not only Christmas trees would burn on Christmas." Some squats in Kreuzberg and the neighboring Neukölln proclaimed themselves "Autonomous Republics." The squatters' movement also benefited from the corruption scandals that delegitimized the SPD/FDP-led Senate. Especially in Kreuzberg and Schöneberg, a political and legal vacuum provided the movement with a lot of space for their activities.

In 1981, the movement grew rapidly under the slogan *Legal, illegal, scheißegal!*, [roughly, "Legal, illegal, it doesn't matter!"]. About three thousand people lived in squats and organized large parts of their daily lives as autonomous collectives. There were a number of

mass demonstrations in support of the squatters; for example, the "Amnesty Demonstration" to Rathaus Schöneberg in June and the "Grunewald Demonstration" to the homes of property speculators. During the Amnesty Demonstration, a supermarket was looted. The bourgeois media spoke of "insurrection" and announced that allied security forces would step in "to keep peace and order in the city" (*Berliner Morgenpost*, July 5, 1981).

The movement answered the police repression with decentralized actions by small groups. Protesting a draconian court sentence against a squatter, they managed to jam the locks of forty banks and smash in the windows of another seventy in two nights—all under the motto, "You Have the Power, We Have the Night!" In addition, there were numerous surprise riots on Kurfürstendamm, Berlin's main shopping street. These caused millions of deutsche marks in damage and led to headlines in the Springer press such as "Berlin Boils in Anger!" The struggles also led to an increased sense of solidarity with other victims of state repression. In March 1981, ten thousand people joined a demonstration in support of the RAF prisoners' hunger strike.

During the initial phase, the booming squatters' movement had very little "theory"—which does not mean that it had no political ideas. Many squatters came from the nondogmatic left-alternative scene and had experiences in antinuclear, student, and prison groups. An early political debate within the movement concerned negotiations with the state. The main argument of the opponents of negotiations was that many squatters were in prison. The main argument of the supporters of negotiations was that houses already occupied and restored needed to be secured. In this context, first media reports about "respectable" squatters appeared to appease the bourgeois public, portraying creative and peaceful people turning rundown buildings into charming alternative homes.

The Concept of Autonomy and the Housing Struggle in West Berlin

Also within the squatters' movement, the term "Autonome" gained increasing popularity. Relevant debates were published in the monthly journal *radikal*. Some Autonome wrote in 1983, "'Autonomy' was a term that seemed to summarize our struggles perfectly. Imported from Italy and presented to our scene in the 'Autonomy Theses' [see

the Appendix], it soon represented everything that was important to us—and still is. Earlier, many of us saw themselves as anarchists, Spontis, or communists, while some had vague, individual ideas about a liberated life. Then we all became Autonome" (no. 123/83).

The "autonomy debate" in *radikal* also made it clear that the Autonomen differed from their autonomous predecessors of the 1968 student revolt. In no. 98/81 comrades wrote: "Turning to Italy's Autonomia movement for help could not solve our identity problem." In the same issue, some self-identified Autonome defined "autonomy" as a demand to "practice different forms of life in the here and now." They continued: "Bourgeois society is no perspective for us. But a different perspective, i.e., a liberated society, cannot exist if we do not take concrete steps toward it by transforming our uneasiness and our destructive tendencies into alternative structures that fulfill our needs and allow for new ways of relating to one another. This demands a cultural revolution." Work was generally rejected, not least because the autonomous structures in Germany had not developed at the workplace. Their basis was rather the common "subculture."

However, some Autonome rejected this definition, as it went too far from a concept of autonomy that meant a collective struggle against wage labor and a political and economic attack against the rule of capital. Indeed, parts of the squatters' movement mainly understood autonomy as an individual retreat from the production process. Apart from the fact that this was an illusionary goal under the objective conditions of capitalism, such an approach also abdicated any attempt to influence society at large.

The individualistic-subjectivist turn of autonomous politics was perhaps most poignantly articulated in a paper entitled "To Stand Still Is the End of Movement" [*Stillstand ist das Ende der Bewegung*], published in *radikal* 1/82 and revisiting the first of the "Autonomous Theses": "We fight for ourselves. We do not engage in representative struggles. We do not fight for ideology, or for the proletariat, or for 'the people.' We fight for a self-determined life."

How could the autonomous movement reach such positions? When the squatters' movement emerged, class conflict in West Germany was hardly visible. Class struggle was no reference point for radical politics, and there was little left but to turn the attention to one's own needs in one's own immediate surroundings—often defined by the alternative movement. In the perception of many autonomous squatters, this was the "real basis" of their struggles: "For the past few years, we, members of the left and alternative scenes, have been working on the creation of structures that enable us to live self-determinedly and to organize our lives collectively. This concerns our economic affairs, our food, our bars, our cultural events, etc. . . . In these spaces of relative freedom, we have the possibility to experiment with communal forms of living and to transform radical experiences into everyday life. Besides, it is inspiring to prove that a different way of life is not only possible but that it actually pays off!"

Some Autonome remained conscious of the dangers of escapism. They criticized the alternative movement accordingly: "Many activists in the alternative scene are only interested in reorganizing their own life, not in fighting the system. They establish social niches and become active only when these niches are threatened. We reject

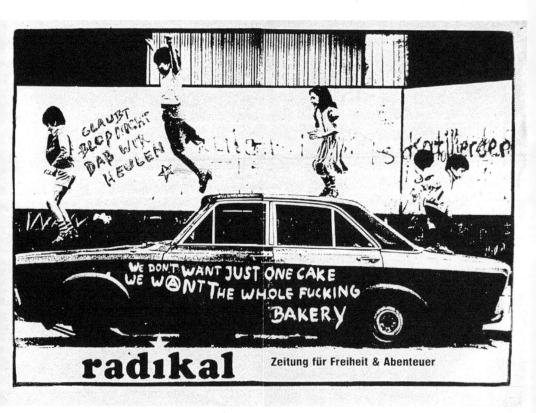

that. Our forms of self-organization should be an integral part of our struggle—they should not be the goal."

A similar critique was formulated with respect to the popular term *Freiraum*, "free space": "We do not criticize the existence of relatively free spaces, but the concept of 'free space' as a goal. To us, free spaces are but departure points for wider struggles. To merely establish and defend them . . . is classical reformism! It poses no challenge to the system. In fact, capitalism proves how flexible it is: 'free spaces' are integrated, resistance is channeled, and ghettos are created that have no explosive force. We are left with nothing but playgrounds."

The End of the Housing Struggle

On September 22, 1981, eight Berlin squats were evicted. Klaus Jürgen Rattay was fatally injured when he was hit by a bus while running from the police. Subsequently, the squatters' movement reached its peak in terms of mobilizing a broad left-liberal spectrum in West Berlin. The state gave the squatters two options: evictions or rent agreements, that is, legalization. The pressure on the movement was mounting, especially because of ever-increasing criminalization: about five thousand people were affected by preliminary investigations.

The alternative and reformist currents within the movement signed agreements to end a conflict with the system and the state they had never been looking for. The opponents of negotiations were increasingly isolated. They criticized the agreements that had been signed but failed to instigate a general housing struggle that included rent strikes and mobilized wider parts of the population. Partly, this was due to new "social housing policies" (an unintended result of the housing struggles) that kept wide parts of the population pacified; partly, it was a result of the individualistic tendencies within the movement. It is also questionable whether the Autonomen could have carried such a struggle at the time—many of its forces were exhausted.

West Berlin's conservative CDU/FDP-led Senate continued its double strategy of integration and repression. This led both to successful evictions and to the restructuring of entire neighborhoods, particularly in Schöneberg. During the peak of the squatters' movement in the summer of 1981, Schöneberg's Winterfeldtplatz was one of the movement's centers and the base for many actions in the city center, which was only three minutes away. Many of the squatters evicted in

Schöneberg went to Kreuzberg where evictions were much less common and legalization more widespread. This was one of the reasons why Kreuzberg turned into a retreat for Autonome and earned its reputation as, in the words of a local CDU politician, a "ghost town of troublemakers."

In the summer of 1984, the last squat was evicted. However, the demise of the squatters' movement did not lead to the demise of the Autonomen. The end of the housing struggles opened up space for new political initiatives, discussions, and campaigns.

THE STRUGGLE AGAINST THE
STARTBAHN-WEST

IN THE FALL OF 1981, THE MOVEMENT against the Startbahn-West—a runway extension at Frankfurt Airport—brought the entire Rhein-Main region to the brink of ungovernability.

The anti-Startbahn movement had begun in the 1970s, as the new runway demanded clear-cuts in a relatively pristine forest. In the beginning, the movement mainly consisted of residents of the affected communities, local politicians of all parties (ranging from the DKP to the CDU), and environmentalist groups. Conventional information campaigns created huge publicity and the first physical protests in the forest were organized. In the area designated for clearing, a village of several wooden cabins was set up, demonstrating the protesters' determination. Many thought that the Startbahn-West could be prevented with peaceful and legal means. All over Hessen, two hundred thousand signatures were collected, although state authorities had already made it clear that they were not interested in the people's opinion. No matter what, the runway had to be built. As a gesture of "good will," however, representatives of BIs were invited to speak at Hessen's parliament about both the ecological consequences and the economic foolishness of the project. Their speeches were received by bored parliamentarians.

The dynamics of the movement changed drastically when the police attacked and destroyed the protesters' village in November 1981. Mass demonstrations and militant confrontations followed: in the forest (along the fence that had now been erected around the construction site), in the inner city, at the airport, on the nearby motorways.

Solidarity events were organized all over the country. In the process, the composition of the movement also changed. At its peak, it included automobile workers from the Opel factories in Rüsselsheim, the entire Frankfurt left, and revolting youths from across the region. It was still dominated, though, by the bourgeois, legalist, and nonviolent groups that wanted to pursue a "democratic" path. The Autonomen emphasized the significance of the runway for NATO and focused on direct action.

When it became clear that the state authorities, including the federal state government and the constitutional court, ignored all petitions and other means of democratic protest, the broad protest movement began to crumble. The legalist and nonviolent activists focused on other issues, such as the looming missile deployment, and formed Green lists for local elections. Meanwhile, the radical currents within the anti-Startbahn movement, especially the Autonomen, prepared the January 1982 "Baulos-2" demonstration. Although Autonome from all over West Germany attended, the demonstration failed to achieve its explicit goal, namely the reoccupation of the construction site. The police presence was too strong.

Although the state authorities secured the construction of the Startbahn in the spring of 1982 with a civil war–like police response to protests that had engulfed an entire region, the resistance never stopped. During the following years, it was mainly organized by re-mainders of the BIs, by individual citizens of the region, and by autonomous groups of the Rhein-Main area. Unlike the regional resistance against the construction of the nuclear power plant in Brokdorf, which collapsed after the defeat at the February 1981 demonstration, the resistance against the Startbahn was kept alive. People met for "Sunday Strolls" [*Sonntagsspaziergänge*] along the construction site every weekend and repeatedly used the occasion for surprise attacks that damaged the security fence more than once.

During this period, the significance of the Startbahn for NATO and the importance of the Frankfurt Airport for the capitalist world market became central themes in the protests, in addition to the ecological aspects. For most protesters, the connections between the resistance against the Startbahn and antiwar and antinuclear struggles were evident.

In April 1984, the Startbahn was to be inaugurated. An "Action Week" in and around Frankfurt was planned. Among the organizers were church groups, social democrats, and Greens. For most of them, the protests meant a final symbolic gesture that would end the chapter. Many BIs and autonomous activists, however, vowed to continue the resistance. The Action Week once again demonstrated the wide range of autonomous politics: it included protests against the Preungesheim prison, legal authorities, and multinational corporations.

Frankfurt Autonome explained: "It will be a long struggle and it will be aimed at the entire social and political system. The success of the struggle will not be measured by how many of our demands will be met, how much property damage we can inflict, or how much air traffic we can disrupt . . . but by how much we can help people escape individualization and alienation, to take control of their lives, and to start fighting" (*BI-Dokumentation*).

Ten thousand people joined the demonstration against the inauguration of the Startbahn, among them many Autonome from all over the country. Even if the opening of the Startbahn was a defeat for the movement, the Action Week demonstrated an encouraging willingness to continue the struggle.

THE ISOLATION OF THE
AUTONOMEN IN THE GERMAN
PEACE MOVEMENT

NEXT TO THE STARTBAHN RESISTANCE and the squatters' movement, the peace movement was the strongest extraparliamentary force in West Germany in the early 1980s. Within the autonomous movement, there were different perspectives on the potential of the peace movement to politicize and radicalize wider parts of the population. The peace movement of the 1960s and early 1970s had mainly been dominated by church groups, pacifists, social democrats, and communists. In the mid-1970s, when the SPD government embraced détente [*Entspannungspolitik*, or "relaxation politics"] and tried to establish a better relationship with Germany's East European neighbors, the peace movement became marginalized. In the late 1970s, however, it experienced an upswing due to NATO plans for several missile bases in West Germany. In the beginning, autonomous groups were not part of the movement.

This changed abruptly when German Army recruits were sworn in during a military ceremony in Bremen's Weserstadion on May 6, 1980. The SPD/FDP coalition government organized a number of such ceremonies to provide a propagandistic boost to its armament plans. In Bremen, a broad left coalition organized a protest. The Autonomen took charge and engaged the police in street battles lasting several hours.

The demonstration in Bremen proved that the autonomous approach to politics—one of the few remaining radical approaches after the German Autumn—was able to connect with a social revolt carried by the country's youth. Subsequent antimilitary demonstrations in Flensburg, Bonn, Hamburg, and other cities confirmed this as much as the squatters' movement.

Within the radical left, the Bremen events triggered discussions about a new anti-imperialist anti-war movement. A regional campaign against the NATO maneuvers near Hildesheim in the fall of 1980 did not bring the expected results. A well-prepared anti-imperialist demonstration could only mobilize about two thousand people and the organizational structures broke apart soon after the event. In Bremen, however, Autonome and other radicals were able to form various "War against War" groups. A lot of their activism was directed at the U.S. Army's second biggest base in Germany, Bremerhaven/Nordenham. (The biggest base was in Frankfurt.)

In 1981–82, Autonome were strongly involved in the organization of three major antiwar actions. In September 1981, there was a demonstration in West Berlin against the visit of the U.S. secretary of state, Alexander Haig, famous for the words, "There are more important things than peace." In the spring of 1982, the Arms Fair IDEE was disrupted in Hanover. And on June 11, 1982, there was another demonstration in West Berlin, this time against the visit of U.S. President Ronald Reagan.

Among these events, the anti-Haig demonstration was the biggest success. After a march of sixty thousand people, about five thousand radicals tried to reach Rathaus Schöneberg to disrupt the official reception. In heavy street-fighting, the police partly lost control. The riots featured prominently in the bourgeois press for days. The demonstration and the clashes had successfully challenged the assumption that West Berlin unanimously embraced the United States as a "protective power" and a "guarantor of peace." This was confirmed by conservative press comments such as the following: "Haig drove through empty streets, protected by police-erected walls right in the middle of West Berlin. The square in front of Schöneberger Rathaus, where the masses once celebrated freedom, appeared like a quarantine zone, the authorities eager to keep people separated rather than united. This, it seemed like, was not the Berlin we knew" (*Die Welt*, September 19, 1981).

What made the Haig demonstration so special? Comrades from Hamburg wrote in a text in 1983:

> The dynamics of the Haig demonstration did not stem from anti-imperialist analyses, but from the social movement of the housing struggle, which formed the demonstration's

"hinterland." Without the housing struggle, events would not have unfolded in the way they did. The experiences that people had made with the system in their everyday life played an important role. The feeling of being personally affected can mobilize folks in very different ways than theoretical analysis or rational insight. The squatters' movement of Berlin gave the demonstration both rear cover and impulse. The fight against imperialism, NATO, and war were all tied into the squatters' movement and made it more than just a single-issue affair. It is fair to ask whether there can ever be an effective radical antiwar movement that is not rooted in everyday social struggles (*Überlegungen zur Anti-Kriegsbewegung*).

These lines hint at a conundrum that the autonomous movement of the early 1980s found itself in: there was a booming peace movement on the one hand, and a weak antiwar movement on the other. During the protests against the Arms Fair in Hanover it came to a split between the Autonomen and wide parts of the peace movement. One month later, autonomous and anti-imperialist groups managed to mobilize five thousand people to join a radical protest against the Reagan visit in West Berlin, but this already happened without the support of other peace movement factions, which, one day earlier, had managed to draw five hundred thousand people to Bonn and one hundred thousand to West Berlin. Although open conflict between the Autonomen and the peace movement could be avoided, autonomous groups found themselves increasingly isolated. There were several reasons for this.

The Autonomen and the anti-war movement had mainly focused on local initiatives and were not able to give the mass movement that emerged in opposition to NATO armament in Germany anti-militaristic and anti-imperialist impulses. Between 1980 and 1982, the radical anti-war movement was marginalized by many organizations and initiatives, including the DKP, the Greens, the Jusos, and most pacifist and church groups. This allowed the peace movement to replace the antiwar movement. Church groups and social democrats became dominant and cemented their role by establishing a central coordination committee in Bonn. Some of these activists took their "leadership role" and the demand to "keep the peace" so seriously that they collaborated with the police when it came to undermine the politics and tactics of the Autonomen.

In 1982–83, comrades from Hamburg tried to establish a wide coordination of autonomous groups in order to strengthen radical resistance against the missile program. Two meetings were organized,

"CREATE PEACE WITHOUT WEAPONS"

one in Hanover in February and one in Lutter in June. Especially the Lutter meeting was strongly affected by the imminent defeat of the New Social Movements (antinuclear, antiwar, squatting). Furthermore, the organizational structures that had been built in preparation for the Reagan demonstration had collapsed shortly after the event, which also led to insufficient support for the arrested and imprisoned. In combination with the isolated position of the Autonomen within the peace movement, these developments demanded reflections on autonomous positions within the left and on future strategies. Some Autonome described the situation thus:

> The situation is similar in many cities: the scene is dispersed, there are hardly any common assemblies and discussions. Groups might form for specific actions (mostly demonstrations), then they break apart. We mainly react to the most ludicrous exploits of the state and add action to action, moving from one issue to the next. . . . There exists very little exchange between the groups working on different topics, there is no common analysis of the current social conditions, and there is no common strategy, which would allow us to determine our goals and means and to establish some kind of continuity in our work (*Vorbereitungsmaterialien*).

The preparation group of the meeting suggested discussing autonomous identity beyond strategic debates about the perspectives of the antiwar movement:

> Aspiring autonomy means first of all to struggle against political and moral alienation in life and work, against the functionalization of other people's interests, and against the internalization of our opponents' morality. It means to reclaim our lives. . . . This is expressed when houses are squatted to live life in dignity and to avoid paying outrageous rent; it is expressed when workers stay at home because they can no longer tolerate the control at the workplace; it is expressed when the unemployed loot supermarkets . . . and when they refuse to support the unions in their mere demand for jobs, which only means integration into a system of oppression and exploitation. Wherever people begin to sabotage the political, moral, and technical structures of domination, an important step toward a self-determined life has been made. Aspiring autonomy also means to engage in public debate with those who think differently and to make the ideas that motivate our life and our actions transparent.

In the summer of 1983, twenty-five thousand people attended a demonstration in Krefeld against the visit of U.S. Vice President George Bush. Autonomous groups organized their own demonstration, which was joined by roughly one thousand comrades. The autonomous protest was quickly stopped and dispersed by special police units. Over 60 people were injured, some heavily, and 138 were arrested. More than 50 of them were sentenced to up to two years in prison.

Large parts of the peace movement clearly distanced themselves from the Autonomen. A "violence debate" followed that isolated the Autonomen even further. Comrades from Hamburg observed that "the term 'autonomous groups' is systematically used by the state to reduce our politics to nothing but the issue of violence." It was increasingly questioned whether any further efforts should be made to collaborate with other factions of the peace movement.

Internal organization also became a much-discussed topic. Autonome had often managed to mobilize nationwide for certain actions. However, the structures that were developed usually disappeared soon after the event. One reason was that any autonomous organization based on regular nationwide meetings faced one and the same accusation, namely to establish top-down organizational structures, which stood in contrast to the most basic autonomous principles. Furthermore, attempts at nationwide organizing were often perceived as substitutes for a lack of local and regional commitment. In the end, no structures were ever established that really went beyond individual events, and after 1983 there was only one serious attempt at doing so, during the IMF campaign from 1986 to 1988.

The peace movement with its strong nonviolent ideology continued to exclude all anti-imperialist and social-revolutionary forces. Their protests—eager to prove their nonviolent commitment—became predictable and empty symbolic gestures of submission to the state. The collaboration with the police also continued. Many peace activists not only wanted to control the Autonomen but were also willing to denounce them.

DEMO 25.6. Krefeld

zum **Seidenweberhaus**

gegen die **Kriegspropaganda** der **NATO**

mit Bush, Kohl, Carstens

Krieg dem imperialistischen Krieg!

da wo wir kämpfen ist das Leben!

10⁰⁰ HBF
Krefeld

autonome und antiimperialistische gruppen

III. A FEW SKETCHES OF THE AUTONOMOUS MOVEMENT DURING THE FINAL YEARS OF THE WEST GERMAN REPUBLIC

DURING AND AFTER THE DISILLUSIONING experiences with the German peace movement, the Autonomen increasingly discussed social-revolutionary perspectives. As far as organizational questions were concerned, they saw themselves in conflict with the Green Party as much as with anti-imperialists and the urban guerrilla. Of special significance were the political and social developments in the centers of the movement—Hamburg, West Berlin, and Frankfurt—and the campaign against the IMF and World Bank Summit in West Berlin. This also reflected a renewed focus of many activists on the big cities. During a couple of years, the focal points of activism had been rural areas and provincial towns, especially in connection with the antinuclear struggles. One of the weaknesses of the period was the inability to connect these struggles to radical politics in the urban centers. This would have made the work of the police more difficult, too. In any case, the radicals had already announced their renewed activism in the cities with the early 1980s squatting wave in West Berlin.

The following sketches of social and political developments—partly caused by the Autonomen themselves, partly entirely outside of their control—are only some examples of the wide array of issues that autonomous activists got involved in during the decade leading up to the fall of the Berlin Wall. A comprehensive overview would have to include chapters on autonomous activism in the Ruhr Valley and in Southern Germany, especially in Freiburg. It would also have to include chapters on the solidarity work for refugees, on antifascist organizing, on campaigns against the gentrification and yuppification of neighborhoods, on debates on sexual violence, and on the autonomous women's movement—activities which all contributed enormously to the development of autonomous politics. Unfortunately, the author can do little more than point out these painful gaps. It needs someone else to engage in the analysis of these struggles, and their failures. This is necessary for a new politics of liberation and a strong autonomous movement on the way to the twenty-first century.

The following presentation traces the "highlights" of autonomous politics in the 1980s—unfortunately, these were often determined by the attention they received in the bourgeois media or by the state repression they triggered. For example, it is unclear how much there would really be to write about the Startbahn protests after 1983 were it not for the fatal—and fatefully wrong—shootings of two policemen in 1987. In any case, the decision made by the author means that many of the less spectacular everyday struggles and debates will be underrepresented. Autonome in Hamburg discussed much more than the Hafenstraße, and Autonome in Kreuzberg much more than the next neighborhood riot. However, the author chose to focus on the "highlights" because they shaped not only the public image of the Autonomen but also their self-understanding; and they contributed significantly to making the Autonomen a symbolic counterinstitution of German society. Whether this is good or bad remains to be seen.

"WOMEN RESIST! PROTEST AGAINST THE CLOSURE OF FRANKFURT'S AUTONOMOUS WOMEN'S SHELTER!"

CLASS MOVEMENTS AND
MASS MOVEMENTS

THE DISAPPOINTING EXPERIENCES with the peace movement in 1983 led many Autonome to a sharp critique of social movements in general. Is it really possible to create revolutionary change by attempting to radicalize social movements? There were many heated discussions about how to maintain the practical radicalism and militancy that the Autonomen became known for while, simultaneously, expanding beyond the confines of a narrow cultural scene. For a period of time, the concept of Temp Workers' Groups [*Jobbergruppen*] seemed promising. These were founded in the early 1980s when the impact of the economic crisis was also felt in the radical scene. The Temp Workers' Groups focused on the activists' role on the labor market. The second "Oil Crisis" of 1979–80 had caused high unemployment in West Germany and allowed the ruling class to implement serious cuts in social services (unemployment benefits, social welfare, student loans, etc.), which had often been the basis of activists' economic survival. The relative economic freedom that characterized the activist scene of the 1970s gave way to new necessities of employment and a lack of social and economic security. As a consequence, many autonomous circles across West Germany and West Berlin formed groups of temporary and unemployed workers and revived notions of the Italian operaismo.

At the first nationwide "Congress of the Unemployed" in 1982, the Temp Workers' Groups were able to prevent the DGB from taking control. However, there was no common ground between the different autonomous groups other than a rejection of the DGB approach of "Jobs for All!" which included, for example, jobs in the nuclear and arms industry. Due to the lack of a common platform, no nationwide movement got off the ground.

The relationship that the Autonomen had to labor issues suffered from the same difficulties that the New Left experienced in relation to the working class in the late 1960s. In the 1980s, wage labor was dominated by a class of politically integrated, unionized, and skilled workers who belonged to so-called core workers' groups, meaning they had relatively secure, long-term employment. They were not very open to autonomous ideas of a "self-determined" life and the fight against capital. Although the number of temporary workers increased significantly during this period, the core workers remained the dominant force among the proletariat. Furthermore, autonomous organizing in the workplace was undermined by the "mobility of the disenfranchised." In other words, many temporary workers preferred to quit when their situation became unbearable over engaging in tedious, and perhaps futile, political organizing. Finally, the Autonomen never found an answer to the ruling class's ability to portray autonomous workers' groups as a threat to core workers' groups—a phenomenon that could be traced back to the 1970s stereotype of the mobile and unreliable activist worker.

Still, throughout the 1980s, there was a remarkable continuity of workplace-related initiatives by autonomous groups and a strong commitment to unemployment issues. The right to live a dignified life was more important than the demands of wage labor. However, it remained difficult for autonomous activists to build alliances in workplaces. The fact that Autonome could always retreat and survive within their own structures distinguished them from other workers. Workplace organizing on the one hand, and the defense of independent structures (a "scene") on the other, proved to be a contradiction that the activists could not solve.

BETWEEN BALACLAVAS
AND BIRKENSTOCKS:
THE AUTONOMOUS MOVEMENT
AND THE GREENS

THE EMERGENCE OF THE GREEN PARTY in the late 1970s happened somewhere in the maze of the New Left, the antinuclear movement, and the collapse of the K-groups. The Greens presented themselves in the beginning as an "antiparty" or a "protest party." Unsurprisingly, the integration into the parliamentary system corrupted most of them. First, the principle of rotation was abandoned, then parliamentarians ignored grassroots decisions citing "individual conscience," and finally the salaries based on the average income of a skilled laborer no longer sufficed to make the life of a parliamentarian bearable—ever bigger chunks of the generous wages paid to parliamentarians went to private bank accounts rather than to the environmental funds that the party had once established for that purpose.

The 1980s were marked by the conflict between the "Fundis" and the "Realos" within the party. The term "Fundi" (short for "fundamentalist") had been coined by the "Realo" ("realistic") wing as a derogatory term suggesting that Green Party members who held on to original principles were narrow-mined, irrational, and unpredictable—a bit like "Islamic fundamentalists." In reality, the Fundi wing consisted mainly of former KB members, who now saw themselves as "eco-socialists," and of "so-called radical ecologists," mainly from Hessen. The Fundis either rejected any collaboration with the established parties (for example, in Frankfurt) or they tried to challenge the SPD with a more radical social democratic program (for example, in Hamburg in 1982 and 1986).

The Realos had given that name to themselves—a clear indication that they, fatalistically, had accepted the status quo. They pursued coalition governments with the SPD at any price. Their program was made to fit the institutional apparatus, which also explains the generous coverage they received in the liberal media. The Realos represented a tendency characteristic of many social movements, namely the belief that a participation in the power structures of bourgeois parliamentarianism will most likely guarantee the movement's preservation—and, especially, the preservation of themselves as the movement's representatives.

In the beginning, the relationship between the Autonomen and the Greens was complex. At times, there were political coalitions, for example, in antinuclear protests or the defense of squatted houses. For the Greens, the Autonomen were often a useful "militant arm" in political struggles. The "militant autonomous threat" strengthened the Greens' position in negotiations with other parties. The CDU Minister of Finance Gerhard Stoltenberg was therefore not completely wrong when he called the Autonomen the "armed wing of the Green Party." The Autonomen, on the other hand, needed the Greens mainly for protection from state repression.

However, this relationship pretty much ended in 1987. Already in 1986, after the clashes in Wackersdorf and Brokdorf, prominent Green parliamentarians wrote an open letter to the antinuclear movement demanding the exclusion of the Autonomen. The reaction of the Green Party to the Kreuzberg riot of May 1, 1987, was similar. After the November 1987 killings of two policemen at the Startbahn-West, the Greens supported the state investigation and the repression targeting the entire autonomous movement. Meanwhile, the Autonomen no longer approached the Greens as possible coalition partners.

In summary, the constitutional state was extremely successful in integrating the Green Party. Some Autonome already stated in 1984 that "if the Greens didn't exist, the state would have to invent them." This is very true. At times, the Green Party mainly served as a tool to transform and conceal bourgeois ideologies of domination.

AUTONOMEN,
ANTI-IMPERIALISTS,
AND THE URBAN GUERRILLA

HE REVOLUTIONARY CELLS CONCEPT of a social-revolutionary grassroots guerrilla resonated more with the self-understanding and the militant praxis of the Autonomen than the RAF concept of an anti-imperialist First World guerrilla. The Revolutionary Cells also relied less on written treatises than the RAF. In the early 1980s, some Autonome saw the Revolutionary Cells as a *Guerriglia diffusa* "close to the movement." This was linked to the demand that the Revolutionary Cells give up their form of organization and join the autonomous movement (see the debates in *radikal* from 1983–84).

In the early 1980s, many Revolutionary Cells actions were clearly related to social movement struggles. For two years, for example, they attacked firms involved in the construction of the Startbahn-West. In the late 1980s, an internationalist and anti-imperialist faction developed within the Revolutionary Cells. Meanwhile, the Rote Zora attacked branches of the Adler clothing company in solidarity with strikes by women workers in the company's South Korean plants.

The RAF had already returned to its anti-imperialist roots after the failed 1977 Offensive. In 1979, the group attacked the NATO Commander Alexander Haig, and, in 1981, the U.S. Army General Frederick Kroesen. It seemed obvious that the RAF tried to relate to the social movements of the period, in particular the antiwar movement. In May 1982, the group published its first position paper in more than half a decade, entitled "Guerrilla, Resistance, and the Anti-imperialist Front in Western Europe." The paper, terribly written, proclaimed a "proletarian internationalism," positively referencing the politics and the role of the Soviet Union, and demanding a common "Front" with the militants of the social movements. The RAF commandos, living underground, should occupy a leading role.

The "Front Paper" strongly influenced the "anti-imps" (anti-imperialists) of the 1980s. In short, the anti-imps were radicals whose politics strongly followed the RAF concept. Like the Autonomen, they saw themselves involved in a revolutionary movement. They organized widespread information, support, and solidarity campaigns for imprisoned RAF comrades. They also joined protests organized by the Autonomen, for example, against the Reagan visit in 1982 or in support of the Hafenstraße squats in the second half of the 1980s. There was also some collaboration, for example, during the RAF prisoners' hunger strikes in 1984–85. In general, though, the political differences between the Autonomen and the anti-imps were too big for close cooperation. The conflicts came to a head when a RAF commando killed a randomly chosen low-level GI during the preparations for an attack on the U.S. Air Force Base in Frankfurt. Many Autonome rejected the action as "counterrevolutionary," while some anti-imps detected a "bankrupt moral-bourgeois humanism" in this reaction. At a congress with one thousand participants organized in Frankfurt in January 1986 under the title "Anti-imperialist and Anti-capitalist Resistance in Western Europe" it came to physical confrontations.

Frankfurt's autonome L.U.P.U.S.-gruppe presented a highly influential critique of the RAF in the fall of 1986. Comparing the initial goals and intentions of the group from the early 1970s to the theory and praxis of the RAF in the 1980s, the authors came to the conclusion that the urban guerrilla concept had failed, not least measured by its own standards: "The guerrilla did not 'expand' or 'take root.' . . . Fact is that more RAF members today are dead, in prison, or in exile than fighting in West Germany. Fact is that the current politics of the RAF are characterized by defeat rather than victory. Fact is that the sympathy that at least some circles had for the RAF fourteen years ago has basically disappeared. Fact is that the RAF feels safer abroad than in the country of its origin—which confirms that the underground here is too shallow to protect them" (*Schwarzer Faden*, no. 24, 1986). The RAF never responded to this critique.

In the mid-1980s, the anti-imps propagated the slogan, "A Front Emerges from a Fighting Movement—Unity in the Fight for Shared Detention!" This was a clear reference to the "Front Paper." The anti-imps tried to connect the struggles of anti-imperialist liberation

ANTIIMPERIALISTISCHER UND ANTIKAPITALISTISCHER WIDERSTAND IN WESTEUROPA

Internationale Diskussions- und Informationstage

FR. 31.1. – DI. 4.2.86 • FRANKFURT • FACHHOCHSCHULE NIBELUNGENALLEE 13 • Beginn: FR. 17.00

mit Genoss/inn/en aus der BRD, Spanien, Italien, Griechenland, Portugal, Irland...
eingeladen sind Anwälte und Angehörige von politischen Gefangenen

movements, First World resistance fighters, and imprisoned anti-imperialist activists. Ranking the "front" higher than the "movement" indicated a shift toward militarism. Within the political framework of the anti-imps, in which the Soviet Union was an ally in the fight against the main enemy, U.S. imperialism, this was logical. More than once, the anti-imps instrumentalized the terrible prison conditions of RAF inmates to support their militaristic and Marxist-Leninist understanding of politics vis-à-vis the Autonomen.

Despite their rejection of the anti-imps' politics, Autonome were very active in solidarity campaigns for RAF prisoners. Partly, this was because many autonomous activists had experienced terrible prison conditions themselves. Partly, it was because, despite all the conflicts, some structures of solidarity between anti-imps and Autonome had been established, especially in Hamburg, where both camps fought side by side in the defense of the Hafenstraße. In summary, the relationship between the Autonomen and the RAF remained ambivalent: while there was strong moral support for the prisoners and their demands, the group's urban guerrilla concept was rejected.

THE ANTINUCLEAR MOVEMENT
OF THE 1980s

THE AUTONOMOUS CRITIQUE OF THE peace movement meant that the Autonomen had changed their perception of social movements in general. Social movements were no longer seen as the only possible arena for social-revolutionary action. However, as not too many other options for mass agitation existed, Autonome remained active in social movements, even if most of these contradicted the radical ambitions of autonomous politics. This was largely a pragmatic decision.

After the big Brokdorf demonstration of 1981, the antinuclear movement had been overshadowed by the peace movement. With the construction of the Brokdorf nuclear power plant despite broad public resistance, the state and the nuclear mafia had managed to break the five-year moratorium on the construction of new nuclear power plants. During the 1980s, the usage of nuclear power in West Germany doubled. Antinuclear protests had mainly become regional affairs, even if, in 1982, there was fairly successful nationwide mobilization for demonstrations in Gorleben, Kalkar, and at Schacht Konrad near Salzgitter. Autonome played an important role in all of these, actively trying to break through the barriers protecting the sites and engaging the police in serious clashes. In Kalkar, these incidents were isolated, but at the September 1982 "Dance on the Volcano" protest in Gorleben there was heavy rioting. For the first time in years, the Autonomen had managed to crack the nonviolence ideology of the local BI. This led to heated discussions but established an autonomous presence in the region. The influence of the Autonomen grew between 1982 and 1985, as an increasing number of autonomous comrades—from the region itself as well as from Hamburg, Hanover, Bremen, and West Berlin—came to Gorleben to protest the start of operations at the nuclear storage facility. The protests were not reduced to this, however. They addressed many related issues. A very effective blend of legal and illegal, nonviolent and militant, open and hidden forms of resistance emerged, directed at the operators, suppliers, and distributors of the nuclear mafia. The high number of sabotage actions and barricades posed enormous challenges for the facility's administration. The "Wendland Blockade" of April 1984 proved that dedicated—and partly also militant—resistance within social movements remained possible as long as there was a sense of basic solidarity.

After the antinuclear movement had regained enough strength in the mid-1980s to step out of the peace movement's shadow, it became a forum where very different radical currents of the extraparliamentary left mingled. This was confirmed by the 1984 Antinuclear National Conference in Braunschweig. Demands to limit resistance to legal and peaceful protests were clearly rejected and there was a strong sense of solidarity for all persecuted antinuclear activists. Participants also formulated a "Call to Action" against the World Economic Summit in the spring of 1985 in Bonn. Radical antinuclear activists and Autonome prepared a broad demonstration against "hunger, exploitation, and imperialism." Thirty thousand people attended, including a significant autonomous bloc.

Wackersdorf

In February 1985, the energy supply companies decided that a nuclear reprocessing plant should be built in Wackersdorf, Bavaria. Autonome were involved in the resistance from the beginning. The "Southern German Autonomen Plenum" was a central force. It had been founded in connections with activities against the 1985 World Economic Summit in Bonn. Many Autonome argued that the reprocessing plant was an indirect way for West German imperialism to acquire nuclear arms. Autonome occupied the construction site and carried out direct action against companies involved in the construction process. All attempts by the police and the conservative local Bürgerinitiative Schwandorf to isolate the Autonomen failed. When the occupiers of the construction site were brutally evicted by SEK units in 1985, there was enormous solidarity among the local population.

The Autonomen had fought hard for the occupation, which had always been eyed skeptically by those favoring legal and bourgeois means of protest. At the end of 1985 and the beginning of 1986, several successful militant actions in Wackersdorf gave an enormous boost to the resistance and inspired many local residents. The usual, and often paralyzing, "violence debate" became meaningless. Although the authorities proceeded with the construction of the plant, resistance did not wane. In the spirit of the Startbahn-West, "Sunday Strolls" were organized along the construction fence. Repeatedly, these allowed for successful attacks on the site. The clashes with the police finally came to a head on Epiphany 1986, only weeks after the nuclear disaster of Chernobyl. For almost three days, locals tried to storm the construction site together with Autonome who had come from all over the country. The protesters succeeded in dismantling significant parts of the allegedly indestructible armored concrete fence. At times, the

police lost complete control over the events and finally attacked the entire demonstration with gas grenades fired from helicopters. In the aftermath, even some CSU members argued for a "pause of reflection." The regional chief of police was fired. The Bavarian government under Franz-Josef Strauß, however, insisted on the completion of the project and practically implemented a state of emergency in the region for several months.

The autonomous groups involved in the Wackersdorf protests tried to answer the intimidation by the state with an expansion of their actions. They targeted not only the construction site, but also the related infrastructure: construction companies, employment agencies, etc. Together with the left wing of the local BIs, they intended to take the resistance from the construction site to the region as a whole. It was important to integrate the everyday life of the local population into the struggle and to raise awareness about who was going to build the reprocessing plant and who was going to profit from it. This new strategy was expressed in the "Action Days" organized in October 1986. The success was limited. First, the Autonomen had reached their limits as "traveling protesters" and the state repression had begun to take its toll. Second, it proved difficult to establish a broad local resistance movement. The political aspirations of the Autonomen appeared too high and could not be achieved, especially for them as "strangers" in the region. Eventually, their claims became mainly rhetoric, as there were no signs of widespread social unrest in the Wackersdorf area. The Autonomen were further weakened by conflicts with the KB and other factions within the antinuclear movement. By 1987, the influence of the autonomous groups on the movement had significantly dwindled. This led to an overall depolitization and a boost for the bourgeois currents.

The Nuclear Disaster of Chernobyl

After the nuclear disaster of Chernobyl in 1986, the antinuclear movement experienced a surge. Nationwide campaigns, which had almost been impossible since 1981, became feasible again. The Epiphany riots in Wackersdorf inspired autonomous groups elsewhere. When the next big Wackersdorf demonstration was announced for June 7, activists also mobilized for a demonstration on the same day in Brokdorf.

rend uns der Atomscheiß von Tschernobyl
noch um die Ohren fliegt
ein neues Atomkraftwerk in Betrieb gehen!

7. 6. 86
BROKDORF
DEMO

Sofortige Stillegung aller Atomanlagen!

The Brokdorf demonstration rekindled a resistance that had basically vanished. It was clear that the Autonomen would play the most important role at the event. Unfortunately, they were no unified force. The only aspect the various autonomous groups were able to agree upon was that they wanted to escalate the situation. This, once again, reduced the "autonomous position" to militant tactics.

A convoy was organized that would travel to Brokdorf from Hamburg. The concept was similar to the one from 1981. The goal was to get as close to the construction fence as possible. If breaking through the police barriers seemed impossible, people were ready to return to Hamburg to do "effective actions" there. However, the police had learned their lesson from five years ago, and the concept failed. When the comrades at the head of the convoy tried to break through an apparently harmless police barrier, all vehicles entered a trap in the remote village of Kleve, far from Brokdorf. SEK units staged a surprise attack on the head of the convoy and basically destroyed all vehicles, some of which burned out. Poor coordination among the protesters meant that ten thousand people at the back of the convoy were unaware of what was happening. They had been tricked by the police without even knowing it. The public image was one of thousands of protesters completely incapable of stopping the police assault. This demoralizing picture was echoed by reports from the construction site where the small group of protesters that had managed to gather there was chased away with CS gas and helicopters. There had been no significant attacks on the fence at all.

One day later, the state authorities struck yet another blow to the antinuclear movement. Eight hundred people who protested the police actions of the previous day were kept in a "kettle," that is, they were surrounded and detained by police, for twelve hours. The SPD-led Senate justified this by citing the "violence" of autonomous activists, although hardly any Autonome were in the kettle. Fortunately, the behavior of the police caused widespread uproar in Hamburg. Three days later, fifty thousand people demonstrated against the nuclear program and state repression. The Autonomen, however, had lost their central role and mainly tried to collect money for their cars.

The failed Brokdorf protest ended the short revival of a militant nationwide antinuclear movement. Even if 150 power poles were taken down in the following months, the government took control of the situation as soon as the immediate fallout of the Chernobyl disaster had passed. Establishing a Ministry for the Environment seemed enough to regain trust and credibility. The radical antinuclear movement became, once again, marginalized.

Summarizing the antinuclear movement between 1982 and 1988, it can be said that, with the exception of Gorleben, it had not been able to disrupt the government's nuclear program in any significant way. The political pressure created by the Chernobyl disaster delayed the beginning of operations in Brokdorf by half a year but did not make a big difference otherwise. However, the antinuclear movement offered, in complete contrast to the peace movement, an infrastructure in which autonomous activists could experiment with different forms of resistance, especially in Gorleben and Wackersdorf. This remained important, despite of the movement's limited success.

28.12. -1.1.
AUFRUHR
HAFENSTR.
Diskussionen + Aktionen z
Widerstand
Unterdrückun
sozialer Verelendun
Faschismus /Antifaschism
Internationali ismu
KONZERTE
FETE
DEMO
31.12.
gegen
KNAST
HAMBURG – STADT DER PFEFFERSÄCKE
NO FUTURE for the SYSTEM
Schweine
21

IN HAMBURG THERE IS A BEAUTIFUL HAFENSTRAßE

THE WEST BERLIN SQUATTERS' MOVEMENT of 1980–81 also inspired activists in Hamburg. Afraid of Berlin-like developments, the Hamburg Senate adopted the so-called Twenty-Four-Hour Rule, which meant that no house in Hamburg was to be occupied for more than twenty-four hours. Accordingly, the Hamburg police crushed all attempts at occupations brutally.

Under these circumstances, open occupations were basically impossible in Hamburg, and activists turned to "secret" or "quiet" occupations. In the fall of 1981, the houses of the Hafenstraße in St. Pauli were occupied that way. The occupations were only made public in the following spring, shortly before the mayoral elections, when the squatters felt they had the political weight to engage in negotiations with the Senate about rent agreements. Fearing riots in the city at an inconvenient time, the Senate granted the squatters the right to stay until the end of 1986.

During the following years, the houses in the Hafenstraße became a center of Hamburg's autonomous and anti-imperialist groups and of political campaigns—for example, the peace movement's activities in the fall of 1983, the support for the hunger strike of RAF prisoners in 1984–85, and the demonstrations after the murder of the antifascist Günter Sare in September 1985, which had a big impact on the city's radical left. Around New Year's 1986, the first *Hafentage*, "Harbour Days," where organized, which would turn into one of the most important annual meetings for Autonome from all of West Germany and beyond. They contributed significantly to making the Hafenstraße a

nationwide, even partly international symbol. The squatters were involved in a variety of political activities. They were a driving force behind the 1986 demonstration in Brokdorf. In many towns—for example, in West Berlin and Cologne—people formed Hafenstraße solidarity groups.

In 1986, there were a number of brutal police attacks on the squats. Their purpose was to prepare the eviction by the end of the year, once the rental agreement had run out. The squatters and other autonomous activists responded with militant actions and instigated a public debate with the help of the newly founded solidarity group Initiative Hafenstraße. In particular, they sought collaboration with neighborhood residents and the broader Hamburg left. On December 20, 1986, ten thousand people marched in support of the Hafenstraße. There was a consensus that no police cordon would be accepted during the demonstration. When the police approached the one-thousand-strong "Revolutionary Bloc," equipped with helmets and clubs, they were chased away. The incident did not split the broad Hafenstraße coalition. The state's attempt to divide the movement by repression had failed.

The demonstration was the final chapter of years of militant action—usually conducted by small groups—in support of the Hafenstraße squats. It secured the squats beyond the end of the rental agreement, at least temporarily. For the first time in many years, Hamburg's left was on the offensive. In the spring of 1987, there were several actions in support of the Hafenstraße all over Hamburg on the so-called Day X. In the summer, some Hafenstraße apartments that had been evicted in 1986 were reoccupied. The squatters increased the pressure on the authorities "to give up their eviction and demolition plans and the terror of the last year," as one of their flyers stated. Throughout 1987, the Hafenstraße squatters and Hamburg's autonomous left set the political agenda in the city. The confidence to withstand a possible police assault with militant resistance grew steadily and the houses were heavily fortified. After long internal debates, it was decided that the houses would be actively defended and that the defense would be properly prepared. This decision was made public and was an explicit aspect of the solidarity campaigns. The courage and the determination of the squatters not to accept police harassment and assault led to the successful "Barricade Days" in November 1987, which forced the politicians to abandon their eviction plans and secured the long-term existence of the Hafenstraße squats. However, the success was dampened by the fact that a rental agreement was signed, violating many regular clauses of tenancy law by tying it to the criminal code. Technically, the entire Hafenstraße could get evicted if one resident nicked a can of beer from a supermarket. While nothing like this has happened so far, the amendments to the agreement serve as a permanent threat to the squats.

IN WEST BERLIN THERE IS A
WONDERFUL KREUZBERG

Despite the demise of the squatters' movement, the Autonomen in West Berlin survived as a political current. Some of them shifted their focus back to antinuclear activism, first in Gorleben, then in Wackersdorf. Others focused on antimilitaristic activism, especially against the ongoing military presence of the Allies. There was an internationalist movement, which organized, for example, the "Coffee Klatsch Campaign" against branches of multinational coffee corporations in Berlin. Labor activism continued as well, with an ongoing focus on temporary and unemployed workers. There were autonomous groups that took a theoretical turn, and a collective continued to produce and distribute the journal *radikal*.

Although there was no common theme in the mid-1980s that brought all the different groups together, the Autonomen gained in strength. There were notable autonomous blocs at all of the bigger radical events in the city—for example, at the South Africa demonstration and at the protests against the visit of the U.S. Secretary of State George P. Shultz in 1985, and at the rallies after the U.S. attack on Libya a year later.

The organizational basis of the autonomous movement consisted of general assemblies. These were often arranged spontaneously and the participants mainly discussed technical matters like demonstration routes and responses to police attacks. Once demonstrations and actions were over, they were hardly ever collectively evaluated. Two attempts—in the summer of 1986 and in early 1987—to establish more regular exchange between autonomous groups in the form of delegate councils failed. The strong autonomous reservations against representative politics and all forms of leadership (subtle or open) could not be overcome.

The Kreuzberg Riot of May 1, 1987

At a time of particularly loose autonomous organization, the Kreuzberg events of May 1, 1987, came as a surprise to everyone. An unpretentious street party developed into a full-scale riot, in which Autonome fought alongside a significant number of Kreuzberg residents. The frustration that had piled up over the years in Kreuzberg 36 literally exploded that night. The police were not able to enter the neighborhood for hours. A "lawless zone" was created, characterized by a festive and jubilant mood. While Autonome kept the police away with strategically placed barricades, many residents engaged in "proletarian shopping." When one supermarket was emptied to the last can of tuna, it was set on fire to the cheers of bystanders.

The neighborhood uprising made several of the city's biggest social and political problems painfully obvious. While the Berlin Senate had managed to crush the squatters' movement, the underlying tensions had not been solved, only dislocated. For over a decade, Kreuzberg had been used as a testing field for all sorts of integration and repression policies. The uprising proved that bureaucratic, top-down measures could not solve any of the social problems, no matter how much money the authorities pumped into them. Besides, many Autonome directly channeled the funds into the movement. Given the Autonomen's central role in the May 1 uprising, the autonomous movement had significantly strengthened its position within the city's left.

As far as the assessment of the uprising was concerned, there were different views among the Autonomen. While some spoke of a "class revolt," others stressed the broad range of people involved. There was also no consensus on how to approach the destruction of property that did not directly belong to or represent the ruling class ("small stores," etc.). Some thought that such discussions were "not important," as they concerned unavoidable fringe phenomena and only distracted from more urgent questions. Others stressed the importance of the Autonomen's status in their own neighborhood. There were also those who simply wanted to "fuck shit up." The crucial issue behind all this was whether Autonome should interfere in spontaneous uprisings.

Was it really appropriate for autonomous activists to establish and implement rules for popular revolts? The question concerned the very identity of autonomous politics: the principle of individual freedom in political organizing stood against the notion of organizing others.

The 1987 Reagan Visit

The May 1 uprising further motivated the Autonomen to play a central part in preparing the protests against the Berlin visit of U.S. President Ronald Reagan. The Autonomen were mainly concerned with the political demands of the protests. However, these remained vague until the end. This was illustrated by two very different autonomous calls for the protests. One, strongly influenced by Frankfurt's L.U.P.U.S. group, called on people to "reclaim social identity and cultural space" during a "Week of Resistance." The perspective was summarized in the term *Hönkel*:

> High, Mr. President! Hönkels invite all rebels, troublemakers, pyromaniacs, temporary workers, occasional shoplifters and looters, outlaws, girls and boys, lesbians, gays, and heterosexuals, as well as the irreformable eroticists of the week to a Hönkel intoxication in Dead Wall City. Hönkels are can openers in the supermarket of life. Not willing to wait until humankind changes, Hönkels pretend that it already happened and live their lives accordingly. While you wait for the President of the United States, we wait for his foes, the declared enemies of everyday life and work. . . . We will shake people's minds with drumfire, eroticize everyday life, and burn the taste of freedom and adventure into the city streets. Hönkel means the refusal to be a victim. Give us everything that life has to offer. Let our forms of struggle and desire, the time and the place, the beginning and the extent, not be determined by them! We begin one week earlier and we will never stop. We appear where no one is expecting us. Fuck the truffles—we want the whole bakery! Hönkel intoxication! (*EA-Doku*).

The cultural-revolutionary orientation of the call, written in the best of Sponti traditions, is obvious. It evokes forms of liberation beyond old and tired slogans and political resistance that cannot be analyzed "objectively"—and perhaps not even articulated clearly.

On the other hand, there was a "Call for an Autonomous and Anti-imperialist Bloc," published shortly before the demonstration. It demanded clear political goals, telling the enemy that the struggle was serious and determined:

> The rulers have never drowned in the tears of the people. . . .
> West Berlin, perhaps more than any other city, represents the
> current economic, technological, and political restructuring
> in the capitalist countries. Its development into a center of
> science and into a testing field for new production and ratio-
> nalization technologies as well as its ever-growing repression
> apparatus defines its reality for the ruling class. This is what
> they want to celebrate. For us, this reality, i.e., the system
> of profit, exploitation, and oppression, means more misery,
> more unemployment, and higher rents in the industrialized
> world as well as the destruction of millions of lives in the
> so-called Third World. . . . We see ourselves as a part of the
> worldwide struggle against imperialism, exploitation, and
> patriarchy. Our hunger for liberation, self-determination,
> and collectivity stands against the fat feasts of the rulers!

It is hard to say which one of the calls managed to motivate more Autonome to attend the protests against Reagan's visit on June 12. In any case, they came to West Berlin from all parts of West Germany. The final preparatory discussions mainly concerned technical questions: Are we going to attack the police barriers? Are we going to wear helmets? And so on.

Fifty thousand people attended the demonstration. The autonomous bloc consisted of roughly four thousand comrades who left a strong impression on both the public and the police. The next day, when Reagan arrived, the Berlin Senate decided to seal off the entire Kreuzberg neighborhood. Essentially, this meant that 170,000 people were under arrest. There was also a twenty-four-hour ban on demonstrations in the Tiergarten area, where Reagan was to give a speech, and in the inner city. All this was sanctioned by the allied forces. In other words, a state of emergency was declared in vast parts of West Berlin.

In the night from June 11 to June 12, there were heavy riots, especially in Kreuzberg 36. Engaged were mainly Autonome who, exactly like the police they battled, did not come from Berlin. The police had anticipated the riots and maintained control throughout, injuring and arresting dozens of protesters. Attempts by local Autonome to stop the skirmishes that were both senseless and dangerous failed. The events

DEMO 31. 10.

11 Uhr · Gerhart-Hauptmann-Platz

SOLIDARITÄT mit der Hafenstraße
Keine Räumung – Schluß mit dem Polizeiterror

Hafenstraße bleibt – Weg mit dem Senatsdiktat
Selbstbestimmt Wohnen und Leben!

of May 1 had created a "Kreuzberg myth" that was very compelling to many West German Autonome who used the neighborhood as a valve to release their frustration and anger. Local activists commented sarcastically: "At Heinrichplatz, Autonome from Munich are battling it out with Bavarian police."

Two aspects of the anti-Reagan protests were of particular importance. One, the concept *Hönkel* inspired many people outside of the autonomous scene to spontaneous, diverse, "anarchistic" actions. Two, the impressive autonomous bloc of June 11 inspired further demonstrations of collective autonomous strength; for example, on October 31, 1987, a march of almost two thousand autonomous activists in Hamburg sent a clear signal to the Senate about what to expect in case of a Hafenstraße eviction.

Autonomous Community Organizing

After the Reagan demonstration, some autonomous groups prioritized community organizing. "Neighborhood palavers" [*Kiezpalaver*] were organized in Kreuzberg 36 to share autonomous ideas with a wider public and to make them challengeable. Many autonomous actions related to housing issues and gentrification. Autonome intended to instigate a broad debate about the restructuring of Kreuzberg. The neighborhood was not only one of the strongholds of the autonomous movement but also of the green-alternative middle class. The Green Party received 30 percent of the district vote. The German news magazine *Der Spiegel* wrote in 1988:

> Urban sociologists say that in cities where "fashion, culture, banks, and high-tech" are thriving . . . yuppies carry the "reurbanization" together with the alternative milieu. The following is what happens in simple terms: first, the intellectual and creative alternative scene appears and establishes an infrastructure of shops, bars, and cultural venues. Then "their successful twin," yuppie culture, enters. . . . The cultural program becomes a drawing card for a highly qualified labor force, modern companies, and foreign visitors. "It offers less to those who already live there than to the ones it aims to attract." The tight relationship between alternative and yuppie interests in the restructuring of neighborhoods is confirmed by an empirical study about "gentrification in the inner city of Hamburg." . . . The study substantiates the

"THERE IS NO BORDER BETWEEN PEOPLES,
ONLY BETWEEN THE TOP AND THE BOTTOM."
(KÖPI SQUAT, BERLIN)

impact of modernization, rent increase, and infrastructure
on neighborhood demographics (*Der Spiegel*, no. 36/88).

Gentrification leads to socially underprivileged classes losing their
homes to a better-earning clientele, especially in the inner cities. The
fight against "yuppification" further deepened the gaps between the
Autonomen, who fought with the lower classes, and the (ex-)alterna-
tive movement. In Hamburg's Schanzenviertel, the conflict came to
a head in 1988, when various groups protested the old theater house
Flora being turned into a commercial cultural center. [Eventually,
the protestors occupied the building successfully and turned it into
the autonomous center Rote Flora, "Red Flora."] In West Berlin,
the conflict escalated twice: first, when an alternative day-care center
was to replace an autonomous children's farm, and then after an action against a luxury restaurant. In the case of the day-care center,
the AL called, for the first time, the police against the Autonomen.
In the case of the legitimate but poorly explained action against the
restaurant, the alternative daily *TAZ* denounced the Autonomen as
a nonpolitical, unpredictable, reckless, and semicriminal "neighborhood mafia." These experiences led to even more independent organizing of the Autonomen. Contacts to reformist organizations almost
ceased completely. This became evident in November 1987, when the
Autonomen—in open defiance of the quagmire of institutionalized
tenants' organizations, neighborhood committees, and the AL—organized a neighborhood protest against property speculation and gentrification. Despite particularly strong intimidation by the police after
the Startbahn shootings, almost three thousand people attended. This
confirmed that there remained hardly any grassroots support for the
institutionalized tenants' organizations in Kreuzberg.

Revolutionary May 1

The successful organization of exclusively autonomous demonstrations laid the foundation for a "Revolutionary May 1" demonstration in Kreuzberg and Neukölln in 1988. It was to be clearly separated
from the DGB events, both politically and physically. While the DGB
march and the final speeches at the Reichstag symbolized the Cold
War era, the Autonomen wanted to gather in the neighborhoods of
everyday social and political conflict. Under the motto "Out to the
Streets on May 1" and the Rosa Luxemburg quote "The Revolution Is

Great, All Else Is Mush," more than eight thousand people were mobilized. The police kept a low profile during the march, but attacked the street party at Lausitzer Platz afterward. The attack was an unprovoked punitive measure against the entire Kreuzberg 36 neighborhood as well as a means of intimidation before the anti-IMF campaign got underway. The cops preyed indiscriminately on all participants of the party and many were brutally beaten.

The Revolutionary May 1 demonstration confirmed that the Autonomen had become the strongest force within West Berlin's left. Only one year later, the AL formed a city coalition government with the SPD.

WRONG SHOTS
AT THE STARTBAHN-WEST

EVEN AFTER OPERATIONS AT THE STARTBAHN-WEST had begun in 1984, the Startbahn resistance defined autonomous activism in the Rhein-Main area. Demonstrations and actions, including ongoing Sunday Strolls, sabotage of the security fence, and militant attacks, never ceased. In the spring of 1987, the burning of straw bales even brought air traffic to a halt for several hours. Hessen's Ministry of the Interior contemplated a general ban on demonstrations and gatherings in the Startbahn forest. Political pressure and legal complications never brought these plans to fruition.

However, the Rhein-Main Autonomen had not been able to turn the resistance into a mass movement. Some autonomous comrades wrote in the Summer 1986 issue of the *Hau Ruck* zine: "We continue with the Sunday Strolls despite a lack of perspective. We are aware of this. They Sunday Strolls are—and will probably remain, at least in the near future—mainly a meeting place for us, an inspiring opportunity to exchange ideas. . . . They have become a ritual that is important to many of us personally. . . . Humans are creatures of habit."

In the fall of 1986, there were intensive discussions among the Rhein-Main Autonomen after a Startbahn opponent had suffered severe injuries in a failed attempt to take down a power pole. Felling power poles was popular within the antinuclear movement and had been adopted by many autonomous activists. There were manuals that made it appear as if you could take down a pole for evening entertainment. This was a grave misconception, as the life-threatening injuries sustained by the comrade in Frankfurt proved. Making matters worse,

300.SONNTAGSSPAZIERGANG
gegen
STARTBAHN WEST

I.11.87

14^{00} SKG–Heim

DEMONSTRATION

gegen die neue

Flughafenerweiterung

6. JAHRESTAG der

HÜTTENDORFRÄUMUNG

MO. 2.11.87

18^{00} SKG–HEIM

FACKELZUG

Keine Startbahn West!
NACHTFLUGVERBOT

the members of the group she was with seemed more concerned with protecting their identities than with securing medical aid as quickly as possible. Some Autonome commented: "This kind of behavior does not only contradict the ideals of liberation from an inhumane system that readily sacrifices human life, but it also undermines the sense of community and solidarity that is crucial for any political action. This kind of behavior is self-destructive" (*Discussion Paper of the Bürgerinitiative against the Startbahn-West*).

Attempts to engage the concerned group in a political discussion and to motivate them to offer self-critical reflections were in vain. Furthermore, many autonomous activists were afraid to address the errors. Some spoke cynically of "victims that every struggle entails." Some, however, insisted on a broad debate about militancy and responsibility. The L.U.P.U.S. group published an important contribution, concluding: "Within the autonomous scene, an understanding of militancy has developed that focuses almost exclusively on violence rather than on the utopia of social counterpower."

The L.U.P.U.S. text served as a basis for fiery discussions at the "Libertarian Days" organized in Frankfurt on Easter 1987 under the motto, "From Social Movements to Social Revolution." Fifteen hundred radicals from across the country discussed their activities and experiences. At the end, several hundred of the participants joined a "Startbahn Stroll." Ironically, many of the militant actions carried out in the process were irresponsible and endangered other comrades. It confirmed that the militancy issue remained unresolved.

Eventually, the developments took a turn that no one had expected. On November 2, 1987, Autonome and some of the remaining anti-Startbahn BIs organized a demonstration to commemorate the victims of the violent eviction of the 1981 construction site occupation. In the course of the demonstration, two policemen were fatally shot and several others wounded. The shootings led to an unprecedented wave of repression against the autonomous movement of the Rhein-Main area, for which it was entirely unprepared. More than two hundred homes were searched, numerous arrest warrants were issued, and several activists imprisoned. Many activists talked to the police, which led to deep mistrust and mutual accusations of treachery. The police used the possibility to threaten people with murder charges for what it was worth. Investigating the actual shootings soon became a side issue. The authorities were out to gather as much information about the movement as possible. Some people made statements that lasted several hours, incriminating others and themselves, although they had absolutely no knowledge regarding the shootings. Consequently, the police was able to solve many cases they had not been able to solve for years, indicting numerous activists for attacks on banks, nuclear companies, and power poles.

Eventually, comrades launched a "Statement Refusal" campaign under the slogan "Anna and Arthur Keep Their Mouths Shut." The initiators of the campaign stated clearly that self-critique was necessary, but that it had to be conducted collectively and internally—not alone with the cops. Unfortunately, the campaign came too late. The statements were not only a result of poor judgment, however. They revealed that the movement had neglected to foster personal and political integrity beyond bourgeois norms and state intimidation.

The shootings also revealed that a convincing concept of mass militancy had been lost. Militancy had always defined the autonomous movement, but particularly after the Startbahn began operating in 1984, it often turned into mere ritual and increasingly into an individual gesture. The shootings at the Startbahn marked a rupture with all the original principles of autonomous politics. They were based on random individual choice. No autonomous assembly ever suggested or legitimized such a step. In this sense, it is also wrong to claim that the shootings were a "logical consequence" of how the autonomous movement had developed. The shootings were neither an expression of the movement nor the inevitable result of its activities. This was not least confirmed by the astonishment with which the news was received by most autonomous activists.

Despite the shock, the state repression, and the outrage of the bourgeois public, the shootings did not end autonomous activism. They rather strengthened the autonomous debate on militancy. The discussions were self-critical but not defeatist. The responsibilities and principles of autonomous activism were revisited and the movement's contradictions and weaknesses analyzed. The following excerpt from a statement written by Autonome in Bonn is one example:

> Two human lives were taken. It is impossible to argue that the state of the Startbahn conflict justified this. The deaths were neither necessary to protect the demonstration nor did they advance the overall struggle—rather, the opposite. The state forces violence upon everyone who opposes the state. In this case, however, the link to liberation was lost. In this case, the violence became an end in itself. We have to ensure

Nach dem Tod von zwei Polizisten an der Startbahn West

LINKE und GEWALT

„Gegengewalt
läuft Gefahr,
zu Gewalt zu werden,
wo die Brutalität
der Polizei das Gesetz
des Handelns bestimmt,
wo ohnmächtige Wut
überlegene Rationalität
ablöst, wo der paramilitärische
Einsatz der Polizei mit
paramilitärischen Mitteln
beantwortet wird."

Ulrike Meinhof, Konkret Mai 1968

Veranstaltung:
Do. 19.11.1987
Uni Hörsaal VI
20.00 Uhr

Autonome Frankfurt
Linke Liste Uni Ffm.
BI gegen Flughafenerweiterung
Libertäres Zentrum
Autonome Liste FH, Ffm.

that no one of us can individually decide that the time has come to shoot. We need to reject the idea that it is the level of violence that defines the radicalness of our struggle. . . . A logic in which the Molotov cocktail is followed by the slingshot and then by the gun leads to an escalation of the struggle that only serves those in power. They are not hurt when one of their mercenaries is killed. . . . The killing of a human being cannot be justified only because he stands on the side of the powerful. Indifference toward human life is characteristic of the system that we fight—we cannot allow it to become characteristic for us. We have not fought hard enough against these tendencies within our movement, and therefore we have to accept political responsibility for what happened. As a consequence, we must intensify the fight against the ways in which the system affects us individually and collectively. At the same time, we must not allow the fact that an inhumane system forces contradictory means on us to keep us from struggling. And we must always be clear in pointing out the ones who carry the ultimate responsibility for the deaths in this struggle, not only ours, but also those of policemen and soldiers. A mercenary is to blame for his death if he sells his service; but even more so, the warlord is to blame who sends him into battle (*2.11.87 Dokumentation*).

The Greens expected the autonomous movement to show remorse, to accept the dogma of nonviolence, and to submit to bourgeois norms. This never happened. It might seem trivial that the Autonomen defended their identity, but it was significant in the given context as it prevented them from being integrated into the politics of the state and the Green Party. Perhaps this was the reason why the Bundestag faction of the Greens released a statement demanding a nationwide manhunt for autonomous activists and a criminalization of the entire movement.

WANN

FREIHEIT für INGRID STROBL

...WENN NICHT JETZT

Weg mit § 129 a

Einstellung aller Ermittlungsverfahren

Aufhebung der Haftbefehle

Abschaffung der Sonderhaftbedingungen

VERANSTALTUNG

ATTACKS ON THE AUTONOMOUS WOMEN'S MOVEMENT

IN DECEMBER 1987, THERE WAS A MASSIVE ATTACK against the autonomous women's movement. Under the pretext of "supporting the terrorist organization Revolutionary Cells," state authorities conducted raids of numerous activists' homes across the nation—especially in the Ruhr Valley and in Hamburg. This led to the arrests of Ulla Penselin and Ingrid Strobl. It also forced several comrades to go underground. If the state's intention was to intimidate the movement, it failed. Support events for the imprisoned comrades were organized immediately, and there was a strong wave of politicization after the authorities accused Ulla and Ingrid of activism in fields deemed "relevant for militant action," such as genetic engineering, population policy, women trafficking, and sex tourism. Attendance at events dealing with these topics was higher than ever. Meanwhile, the police met a wall of silence in their investigations. Only the threat of coercive detention could extort some witness statements—they were all useless. Ulla Penselin had to be released after eight months. Meanwhile, the ongoing support for Ingrid Strobl went far beyond the autonomous women's movement. The solidarity campaigns for Ingrid proved how the methods of state repression—namely, isolation, deterrence, and intimidation—can be confronted effectively if our political consciousness is strong enough.

EAT THE RICH!

IWF

BERLIN
Aktionstage
26.9. – 29.9.88
DEMO
29.9. 17⁰⁰
Winterfeldplz.

Nürnberg

15.9. 21⁰⁰ Disco und Infos vor den
        AKTIONSTAGEN IN BERLIN
16.9. 19⁰⁰ Imperialismus – IWF
      21⁰⁰ Fest
17.9. 10⁰⁰ ★Frühstücksspektakel
      19⁰⁰ Bevölkerungspolitik und
      Gentechnologie

im KOMM Königstr.

Autonome Nbg./Erlg.

THE IMF AND
WORLD BANK SUMMIT

THE BIGGEST AUTONOMOUS CAMPAIGN from 1986 to 1988 was the one against the IMF and World Bank Summit in West Berlin. It was characterized by a number of internal conflicts, not least the question of patriarchal structures within the movement. It was never possible to find common ground for strong and unified mobilization. The slogan "Stop the Summit" appeared radical. However, many seemed fine with trying to "stop" the summit when it was already underway, rather than before it even started.

The campaign also revealed strong regional differences between autonomous groups. In some towns, the Autonomen worked together with various factions of the left, while the Autonomen in West Berlin refused to collaborate in any way with the "reformists." For many activists outside of Berlin, the significance of the IMF Summit also remained largely symbolic. In Berlin, fourteen thousand IMF henchmen and an enormous police apparatus were expected. In West Germany, the immediate impact of the IMF Summit—and of IMF policies in general—was rather limited. Eventually, there were various regional protests in September 1988 (in Neumünster, Hamburg, Wuppertal, Frankfurt, Stuttgart, Munich, and other towns) next to the ambitious "Action Days" in West Berlin.

The Action Days had an impressive program and ended with an "International Revolutionary March" of eight thousand people. While this can count as a success, the IMF Summit itself was never really threatened, which stood in stark contrast to the "Stop the Summit" ambitions. Whether different forms of organizing and mobilizing could have brought different results is an open question. In any case, the Action Days revealed that the security forces were far from controlling the entire city during the summit—an assumption that many activists had made. One can only learn from this.

1989

THIS CHAPTER IS INCLUDED FOR ONE REASON ONLY: the year 1989 marked the end of the (West) Federal Republic of Germany, a country that had been founded only forty years earlier by the Western Allies. It was a remarkable event for revolutionaries: suddenly, the state one had fought and rejected for many years just disappeared. And it did so in a way that no one had deemed possible just months earlier. However, even in politics things sometimes happen fast, and not in ways that you would have expected. There is an important lesson to be learned from the fact that anyone who had prophesied the imminent end of both West and East Germany in early 1989 would have been called a crazy fool: namely, to pay more attention to the views of crazy fools.

The activities of the Autonomen in 1989 covered a wide range of issues. In Hamburg, the exemplary comrade Fritz, editor of the autonomous journal *Sabot*, was sentenced to one year in prison in a §129a trial ["membership in a terrorist organization"] because of a stupid press law affair. Damn! In Essen, ten thousand people marched for the immediate release of Ingrid Strobl. Meanwhile, Autonome and anti-imps supported a two-month hunger strike by RAF prisoners who were still fighting for shared detention (the hunger strike was called off when two prisoners were about to die, once again without having secured any major concessions from the state). A strong and youthful Antifa movement emerged after the successes in various elections by the right-wing Republikaner. Third-generation migrants founded their first independent organizations. And the exact meaning of the term "autonomy" was still discussed, now increasingly in relation to "anti-fascism," "racism," and "anti-Semitism."

In Kreuzberg and Neukölln, a second "Revolutionary May 1" demonstration saw serious clashes between protesters and police as well as "proletarian shopping." The events caused the few members of the left-alternative middle class who had not yet distanced themselves from the Autonomen to do so. Even within the autonomous movement, not everyone was happy with the riots despite the victory over the cops due to superior street-fighting tactics. Comrades criticized the "cold technological execution" of the riots and the lack of irony, passion, and laughter. Meanwhile, in Hamburg, the Senate still sent the police to harass the residents of the Hafenstraße. This resulted not only in several solidarity demonstrations, but also in a Senate member having his nose broken.

Probably things would have continued like this, had not the Berlin Wall suddenly come down. And then nothing remained the same. Together with the rest of the West German population—whom they otherwise shared so little with—the Autonomen were rubbing their eyes, unsure of what exactly they were witnessing. Eventually, it was time to ask the big question: "What now?" It seemed clear that coming to the defense of disappearing nation-states was not very autonomous. But was there anything else to do?

Due to the apparent importance of the events, a demonstration on Kurfürstendamm was hastily organized. Only a few days after the wall's collapse, tens of thousands of East Germans marveling at the Kurfürstendamm's glittery consumer kitsch were thus treated to a demonstration of West Berlin Autonome who were friendly enough to greet them with slogans like:

"Money Is Not Enough, Take the Banks!"
(A reference to the "welcome money" that all East Germans received the first time they visited West Berlin or West Germany.)

"No Kohl, No Krenz, No Fatherland!"
(Helmut Kohl was the West German Chancellor, Egon Krenz the East German Chairman of the Council of State.)

"In the West They Are Smarter: Their Wall Is Money!"

Half a decade later, at least the last slogan, improvised during the demonstration, has not lost its relevance.

APPENDIX:
"AUTONOMOUS THESES 1981"

IN 1981, SOME AUTONOMOUS ACTIVISTS who attended a meeting in Padua, Italy, formulated eight theses that tried to capture the most common characteristics of the diverse crowd of activists that had begun to call themselves "Autonome." The theses were never formalized, and different revised and updated versions have appeared—for example, in *radikal* no. 97 extra (August 1981) and in the 1995 reader *Der Stand der Bewegung* (see the afterword)—but to this day the straightforward convictions and sentiments listed in the original paper remain at the core of autonomous identity, even if every single one of them has been passionately discussed and, at times, decidedly rejected by parts of the movement.

1. We fight for ourselves and others fight for themselves. However, connecting our struggles makes us all stronger. We do not engage in "representative struggles." Our activities are based on our own affectedness, "politics of the first person." We do not fight for ideology, or for the proletariat, or for "the people." We fight for a self-determined life in all aspects of our existence, knowing that we can only be free if all are free.

2. We do not engage in dialogue with those in power! We only formulate demands. Those in power can heed them or not.

3. We have not found one another at the workplace. Engaging in wage labor is an exception for us. We have found one another through punk, the "scene," and the subculture we move in.

4. We all embrace a "vague anarchism" but we are not anarchists in a traditional sense. Some of us see communism/Marxism as an ideology of order and domination—an ideology that supports the state while we reject it. Others believe in an "original" communist idea that has been distorted. All of us, however, have great problems with the term "communism" due to the experiences with the K-groups, East Germany, etc.

5. No power to no one! This also means "no power to the workers," "no power to the people," and "no counterpower." No power to no one!

6. Our ideas are very different from those of the alternative movement, but we use the alternative movement's infrastructure. We are aware that capitalism is using the alternative scene to create a new cycle of capital and labor, both by providing employment for unemployed youth and as a testing field for solving economic problems and pacifying social tensions.

7. We are uncertain whether we want a revolt or a revolution. Some want a "permanent revolution," but others say that this wouldn't be any different from a "permanent revolt." Those who mistrust the term "revolution" think it suggests freedom to be realized at a certain point in time, while they don't believe that this is possible. According to them, freedom is the short moment between throwing a rock and the rock hitting its target. However, we all agree that, in the first place, we want to dismantle and to destroy—to formulate affirmative ideals is not our priority.

8. We have no organization per se. Our forms of organization are all more or less spontaneous. There are squatters' councils, telephone chains, autonomous assemblies, and many, many small groups. Short-term groups form to carry out an action or to attend a protests. Long-term groups form to work on continuous projects like radikal, Radio Utopia, or very illegal actions. There aren't any structures more solid than that, no parties and the like, and there is no hierarchy either. To

this day, the movement has not produced any individual representative, spokesperson, or celebrity, that is, no Negri, Dutschke, Cohn Bendit, etc.

LARGE BANNER:
AINST OBEDIENCE, QUIET AND ORDER AS THE ONLY EXPRESSIONS OF LIFE —
AGAINST PASSIVE SUBMISSION — FOR A SELF—DETERMINED LIFE"

SMALL BANNER:
"WHO DOES NOT DARE TO DREAM HAS NO POWER TO FIGHT"

AFTERWORD
BY GABRIEL KUHN

G ERONIMO'S *FEUER UND FLAMME* IS A LEGENDARY book within the radical German-speaking left. When the original edition appeared in
1990, it was not only the first history of the autonomous movement,
but also the first theoretical assessment of its strengths and weaknesses.
It triggered heated debates, some of which were documented in *Feuer
und Flamme 2. Kritiken, Reflexionen und Anmerkungen zur Lage der Autonomen*
[Fire and flames 2: critiques, reflections, and commentaries on the au-
tonomen], a collection of texts inspired by the book and edited by
Geronimo and unnamed comrades in 1992. In 1997, Geronimo added *Glut & Asche. Reflexionen zur Politik der autonomen Bewegung* [Embers
and ashes: reflections on the autonomous movement's politics] to the
previous volumes but the book never achieved the significance of *Feuer
und Flamme*. In 1995, an updated and expanded edition of *Feuer and
Flamme* appeared, which this translation is based on.

Feuer und Flamme was published at a pivotal point in German history. As Geronimo hints at in the final chapter, the reunification of
Germany changed the country's political landscape significantly and
hence also autonomous priorities and possibilities. It has even been
claimed that the autonomous movement ended with the reunification
of Germany, but it is difficult to uphold such a claim. The autonomous
movement was never clearly defined and always based on radical activists identifying themselves as "Autonome." This self-identification remains—there are still numerous "autonomous centers," "autonomous
groups," etc.—even if the forms of autonomous politics might have
changed. In fact, with Autonomy Congresses organized in Hamburg

in 2009 and in Cologne in 2011 and a resurgence of "autonomous general assemblies" [*Autonome Vollversammlungen*] in urban and regional centers, there has been renewed interest in the autonomous movement, also among young activists. Maybe there is a breakthrough looming for the Autonomen in the near future after all? The continuation of the movement's thirty-year history will show.

Parts of this history have been presented and analyzed in a number of books published since the release of *Feuer und Flamme*. In 1997, long-standing leftist publisher Konkret Verlag released *Die Autonomen. Ursprünge, Entwicklung und Profil der autonomen Bewegung* [The Autonomen: origins, development, and profile of the autonomous movement], a well-researched account by Almut Gross and Thomas Schultze. In 2001, Jan Schwarzenmeier self-published *Die Autonomen zwischen Subkultur und sozialer Bewegung* [The Autonomen between sub-culture and social movement], a book focusing on the history of the movement in one of its strongholds, the northern German university town of Göttingen. In 2004, Berlin's Assoziation A released *Autonome in Bewegung: die ersten 23 Jahre* [Autonome in motion: the first 23 years], a superbly illustrated and designed collection of anecdotes, this time centered in Berlin. An informative chapter on the autonomous movement in Austria is included in Robert Foltin's *Und wir bewegen uns doch. Soziale Bewegungen in Österreich* [We do move: social movements in Austria], published by Edition Grundrisse in 2004. Unfortunately, the unique and multifaceted history of the autonomous movement in Switzerland still awaits its documentation in book form.

As far as theoretical reflections go, the most notable titles were published in the 1990s by Frankfurt's autonome L.U.P.U.S.-gruppe: *Geschichte, Rassismus und das Boot – Wessen Kampf gegen welche Verhältnisse?* [History, racism, and the boat: whose struggle against which conditions?] (1992) and *Lichterketten und andere Irrlichter. Texte gegen finstere Zeiten* [Vigils and other ghost lights: texts against dark times] (1994) included essential contributions to the autonomous debates of the 1990s and remain important reference points to this day. In 2001, L.U.P.U.S. published its last text collection, *Die Hunde bellen . . . Von A – RZ. Eine Zeitreise durch die 68er Revolte und die militanten Kämpfe der 70er bis 90er Jahre* [The Dogs Are Barking . . . From A to RZ: time traveling from the 1968 revolt to the militant struggles of the 1970s, '80s, and '90s] (2001), a critical reflection on the goals and tactics of autonomous politics. L.U.P.U.S. also contributed to the influential book *Drei zu Eins* [Three to one] (1991), whose title essay by former 2nd of June Movement member Klaus Viehmann and comrades introduced the concept of "triple oppression" to the radical German left.

There are two books that have collected the voices of numerous autonomous activists. On the occasion of the 1995 Autonomy Congress in Berlin, a group of comrades self-published *Der Stand der Bewegung. 18 Gespräche über linksradikale Politik* [The state of the movement: eighteen conversations on radical left politics]. In 2010, Unrast Verlag published *Perspektiven autonomer Politik* [Perspectives on autonomous politics], a collection of articles and interviews by contemporary autonomous activists contemplating the movement's history, current state, and future possibilities.

The preferred outlets for autonomous debating (and arguing) were the periodicals related to the movement. There have been countless autonomous journals over the years, but *radikal* and *Interim* must count as the two most important. Both experienced a long history of criminalization and repression, documented in the book *20 Jahre radikal. Geschichte und Perspektive autonomer Medien* [Twenty years "radical": history and perspectives of autonomous media], copublished in 1996 by a number of radical German publishing houses. After *radikal* had been on hiatus for years, a few issues have been released since 2005. However, they bear little resemblance to the discussion forum the journal once was. The future of the project remains open. *Interim* still appears biweekly in Berlin.

* * *

The autonomous movement has certainly lost momentum since its heyday in the 1980s, when hundreds of squats seemed to promise the dawn of a new society, when black blocs could consist of thousands, and when the iconic face of a masked autonomous activist appeared on the cover of *Der Spiegel*, Germany's most prominent news magazine. However, the movement never disappeared as an important political factor. As George Katsiaficas points out in his introduction, new focuses arrived in the 1990s, especially due to the rise of nationalist and neofascist sentiments in the wake of German reunification, both in government offices and on the streets. While squatting and, especially, antinuclear activism remained important, autonomous activists were now mainly engaged in fighting the extreme right and state racism. Antisexism and antihomophobia struggles, self-admittedly neglected in Geronimo's account, also remained important throughout the 1990s, as well as issues related to gentrification. The 1995 Autonomy Congress in Berlin, which drew several thousand participants, served as an indication of the ongoing relevance of the autonomous movement.

The late 1990s might have marked a low point in the movement's history, as it was not able to set a political agenda or intervene in social conflicts. Furthermore, it was weakened by bitter infighting. Nonetheless, even during this period, autonomous activists remained an important factor in a number of struggles, most notably antifascism and antinuclear resistance.

The Western alter-globalization movement instigated by the 1999 Seattle protests—whose infamous black bloc was inspired by years of autonomous resistance in the German-speaking world—invigorated the autonomous scene. During Europe's "Summer of Resistance" in 2001, mainly defined by the antineoliberal mass protests in Gothenburg, Prague, and Genoa, Autonome were highly visible. In 2007, a very strong showing at the anti-G8 protests in Rostock/Heiligendamm confirmed their perseverance.

Today, the autonomous movement shows both continuity and innovation. Out of the campaigns, activities, and characteristics featured in *Feuer und Flamme*, the following still constitute key elements of its politics:

"FREE SPACES" AND SQUATTING

The fight for "free" or "autonomous" spaces remains essential. The parameters have changed, not least due to the aggressive persecution of the squatters' movement in the 1980s, but Autonomous Centers [*Autonome Zentren*] all across the German-speaking world provide an impressive infrastructure for radical activists, legalized housing collectives [*Wohnprojekte*] continue to pursue the dream of alternative communal living (albeit today often criticized as "reformist"), and *Wagenburgen*—literally "wagon fortresses": encampments of old caravans, camper vans, house trucks, etc.—beautify just about every town with a noticeable radical community. There has also been a recent squatting revival, with struggles in smaller towns like Münster or Erfurt drawing a lot of attention. While still sometimes denounced as "escapist," "elitist," or even "bourgeois," the struggle for autonomous spaces to experiment with alternative forms of living and organizing remains a defining aspect of autonomous identity.

ANTINUCLEAR STRUGGLES

Geronimo dedicates a lot of room to antinuclear resistance in his book. While this is partly a reflection of his personal political background, it is also an indication of the historical importance of these struggles for the Autonomen. Antinuclear struggles have not only galvanized the autonomous movement throughout its thirty-year history, they have also brought it closest to other grassroots activists and broader networks of resistance. This holds true today.

Since the mid-1990s, autonomous antinuclear resistance has largely focused on the interim nuclear waste storage facility in Gorleben. Every year, a couple of thousand Autonomen join local farmers, environmentalists, and peace activists in disrupting the rail delivery of nuclear waste from a reprocessing plant in France. The unceasing protests have left a mark on the region as a whole. A number of Autonome have taken up residence in the area, commonly known as Wendland, which provides one of the most interesting case studies of autonomous activities reaching beyond the confines of a political subculture and altering the everyday life of entire communities.

MILITANCY

As *Feuer und Flamme* reflects, the autonomous movement has always been associated with militant activism. The *Hasskappe* [literally "hate cap," a black balaclava], the black bloc, and sympathies for the urban guerrilla struggles of the 1970s and 1980s belong to its defining features. In fact, in the public eye the movement has often been reduced to these aspects. While this is clearly simplistic and while there have been numerous self-critical discussions about the possibilities and limitations of militant protest, speaking of "pacifist Autonome" still seems to be a contradiction in itself. In fact, there has been a notable increase in militant actions in recent years. For example, nightly arson attacks on luxury vehicles have become commonplace in Berlin and Hamburg. There have also been daring attacks on military targets related to the deployment of German troops abroad, on government institutions held responsible both for racist migration policies and for the dismantling of social services, and on police stations where particularly extreme incidents of police violence have occurred. In October 2009, three alleged members of the militante gruppe (mg)—which had significant support in the autonomous scene—were sentenced to prison terms of several years for a series of well-publicized attacks.

A few other issues that have characterized autonomous politics for a long time but have not been given much room in Geronimo's account (either because he saw them as less important or because they only became more important later) are antifascism, antisexism, and antiracism.

ANTIFASCISM

Antifascist ("Antifa") groups appeared all across Germany, and beyond, in the early 1990s, after the country's reunification had propelled nationalist and racist sentiments to new heights. Neo-Nazi and neo-fascist street gangs became ever more present and increasingly violent. Extreme right-wing parties entered city councils and provincial parliaments, and the political center moved toward positions that would have been considered clearly right-wing just a decade earlier. Many on the radical left feared an overall drift toward fascism and initiated resistance that ranged from denouncing racist rhetoric to physical self-defense. While these activities had certain success in the 1990s, the struggle is far from over. Extreme right-wing tendencies remain strong in the German-speaking world, and there are several "nationally liberated zones," in which migrants, punks, leftist activists, and whoever else doesn't fit the picture find it unsafe to walk.

Antifa politics today includes painstaking documentation of right-wing activities as much as coalitions with liberal antifascist groups and organizations. Antifa has become such an important factor in autonomous politics that it is often seen as a synonym by the wider public. While this is certainly exaggerated and while it denies the movement's diversity, many young activists do first get in touch with autonomous politics through Antifa groups.

ANTISEXISM

The autonomous women's movement has a long history, and critiques of male dominance, patriarchal structures, and sexist behavior have often been directed at men within the scene itself. Accordingly, women's groups have repeatedly pulled out of "mixed" contexts in order to live, work, and organize independently. Gender issues remain at the forefront of autonomous debates today and are passionately discussed at any bigger autonomous gathering. Many initiatives—from antisexist information campaigns via antipatriarchal men's groups to

gender workshops—attest to the subject's continuing urgency. In recent years, queer culture has been of increasing influence.

ANTIRACISM

In connection both with the rise of nationalism and racism in the
reunified Germany and the ever-growing focus on migration as a key
issue in European politics, antiracist ("Antira") struggles became central for the autonomous movement in the early 1990s and have been
at its core since then. Often overlapping with antifascist politics, antiracist politics are distinguished by a focus on both the specifically racist
elements of fascist culture and the structural racism implemented and
endorsed by European governments. In practical terms, Antira politics
often concentrate on support for non-European migrants as the most
immediate victims of European racism—as targets both of neofascist
street violence and of state-administered migration policies.

Whether any of these issues have caused rifts within the autonomous movement—as some claim—is up to debate. One development
has done so with certainty.

In the early 1990s, once again in the context of German reunification, some groups within the radical left demanded a reexamination
of Germany's history and the left's notion of anti-imperialism, especially in connection with the Israel/Palestine conflict and the notions
of anti-Semitism and anti-Zionism. Out of these debates emerged
the so-called Anti-Germans [*Antideutsche*] who rejected classic anti-
imperialist notions as naïve and reactionary, interpreted anti-Zionism
as concealed anti-Semitism, considered "personalized" critiques of
capitalism ("the evil capitalist!") simplified and crypto-anti-Semitic,
and understood traditional enlightenment values—individual liberty,
secularism, social equality—as necessary steps toward communism.
Their staunch defense of the state of Israel as a safe haven for the
global Jewish community and a guarantor of democratic progress
led, perhaps ironically for an unbending antinationalist movement, to
parading Israeli flags at protests, often accompanied by the flags of
the World War II Allies—the Soviet Flag, the Tricolore, the Union
Jack, and, most commonly, the Stars and Stripes—purportedly as a
means of provocation. In the worst cases, Islamophobia and bellicism
ran rampant. On the other side of the spectrum, anti-imps (portrayed
in Geronimo's account) have shown open support for Hamas and
Hezbollah and hailed figures like Mahmoud Ahmadinejad as important allies in the fight against U.S. imperialism. While far from all the

groups involved in these tendencies considered themselves a part of the autonomous movement, the conflicts had an enormous impact on the scene, ruining friendships, splitting autonomous centers, and even leading to physical confrontations. Today, however, many autonomous activists have grown tired of the situation and a more encouraging future seems in sight.

Issues that have risen to new prominence in the autonomous movement in recent years are animal rights and climate change. Gentrification has steadily increased in importance. Most of the arson attacks on luxury vehicles are related to the issue. There has also been a growing focus on state repression, surveillance, and militarization— all related to the "War on Terror" and the ever-expanding domestic and international security apparatus.

Anticapitalist resistance has not been among the movement's strong points in recent years. While it is true that the mass protests against WTO or G8 summits have helped revitalize the movement in the last decade, Autonome have failed to advance radical anticapitalism despite Germany's ongoing economic crisis and the global financial meltdown. There are some initiatives, like "Payday!" [*Zahltag!*], that have successfully organized protests at government employment agencies and unemployment offices, but in general the autonomous response to the crisis has been weak. This is, of course, not exclusive to the autonomous movement: the entire German left has had difficulties in presenting viable alternatives.

Apart from the inability to turn pressing social issues to political advantage, the autonomous movement has been criticized for various other shortcomings over the years. It has been accused of appearing exclusive and elitist, of lacking theory, of being urban and middle class, of glorifying militancy, and of being "lifestylist." It has also been called a "one generation movement" due to the very high turnover of activists. Much of this criticism is valid. At the same time, there has always been critical self-reflection and serious efforts have been made to progress as a movement. Arguably, this constitutes one of the movement's strengths and is one of the reasons why it has survived for over thirty years.

A special challenge that has recently arisen is the cooptation of autonomous slogans, symbols, tactics, and themes by right-wing youths. The so-called Autonomous Nationalists [Autonome Nationalisten] wear sneakers, baggy pants, and hooded sweatshirts, sport piercings and tribal tattoos, form black blocs, support environmental and animal-rights causes, and change the "Good Night, White Pride" slogan into "Good Night, Left Side" while keeping the same logo. They also claim opposition to centralized party structures and try to present a "hip" version of Nazism. While the phenomenon has caused much confusion and soul-searching within autonomous circles, the boundaries are clearly drawn. Whether the Autonomous Nationalists will remain a fad among the right-wing youth or whether they will establish themselves as a lasting subculture remains to be seen.

Internationally, the autonomous movement has sometimes acquired mythical dimensions. This might be flattering, but myth and reality are two different things. There is no denying that the autonomous movement has its share of contradictions and flaws. Most importantly, though, it persists. Regardless of all the shortcomings and the challenges it has been facing, the German autonomous movement constitutes indeed a unique chapter in the history of the European radical left. It has developed enduring political principles, a well-established infrastructure, and a lasting cultural identity without party structures, theoretical canons, or pledges of allegiance. Many similar movements disappear within a few years or survive only in the form of small "vanguards" that turn dogmatic and sectarian. The Autonomen have defied this logic. Even as they enter their fourth decade, neither centralization nor homogeny is anywhere in sight. Geronimo tells us about their beginnings. Hopefully, no one will have to tell us about their end anytime soon.

G ERONIMO IS A MECHANIC, UNION MEMBER, and longtime autonomous activist living in Hamburg and Berlin. Initiated by the antinuclear and antimilitarist struggles of the 1980s, he continues to be
active in various autonomous campaigns to this day. He has also published extensively under his given name.

G ABRIEL KUHN IS AN AUSTRIAN-BORN author and translator, politi-
cized in the German autonomous movement of the late 1980s.
He worked with the Austrian autonomous journal *TATblatt* in the
1990s. Living in Sweden since 2007, he remains closely connected to
the movement.

G EORGE KATSIAFICAS IS AUTHOR OR EDITOR of eleven books, including ones on the global uprising of 1968 and European and
Asian social movements. Together with Kathleen Cleaver, he coed-
ited *Liberation, Imagination, and the Black Panther Party*. A longtime activist
for peace and justice, he is International Coordinator of the May 18
Institute sat Chonnam National University in Gwangju, South Korea,
and is based at Wentworth Institute of Technology in Boston. His web
site: http://www.eroseffect.com

BECOME A FRIEND OF

These are indisputably momentous times – the financial system is melting down globally and the Empire is stumbling. Now more than ever there is a vital need for radical ideas.

In the four years since its founding—and on a mere shoestring—PM Press has risen to the formidable challenge of publishing and distributing knowledge and entertainment for the struggles ahead. With over 175 releases to date, we have published an impressive and stimulating array of literature, art, music, politics, and culture. Using every available medium, we've succeeded in connecting those hungry for ideas and information to those putting them into practice.

Friends of PM allows you to directly help impact, amplify, and revitalize the discourse and actions of radical writers, filmmakers, and artists. It provides us with a stable foundation from which we can build upon our early successes and provides a much-needed subsidy for the materials that can't necessarily pay their own way. You can help make that happen —and receive every new title automatically delivered to your door once a month—by joining as a Friend of PM Press. And, we'll throw in a free T-Shirt when you sign up.

Here are your options:

- $25 a month: Get all books and pamphlets plus 50% discount on all webstore purchases
- $40 a month: Get all PM Press releases (including CDs and DVDs) plus 50% discount on all webstore purchases
- $100 a month: Superstar—Everything plus PM merchandise, free downloads, and 50% discount on all webstore purchases

For those who can't afford $25 or more a month, we're introducing Sustainer Rates at $15, $10 and $5. Sustainers get a free PM Press t-shirt and a 50% discount on all purchases from our website.

Your Visa or Mastercard will be billed once a month, until you tell us to stop. Or until our efforts succeed in bringing the revolution around. Or the financial meltdown of Capital makes plastic redundant. Whichever comes first.

PM Press was founded at the end of 2007 by a small collection of folks with decades of publishing, media, and organizing experience. PM Press co-conspirators have published and distributed hundreds of books, pamphlets, CDs, and DVDs. Members of PM have founded enduring book fairs, spearheaded victorious tenant organizing campaigns, and worked closely with bookstores, academic conferences, and even rock bands to deliver political and challenging ideas to all walks of life. We're old enough to know what we're doing and young enough to know what's at stake.

We seek to create radical and stimulating fiction and non-fiction books, pamphlets, t-shirts, visual and audio materials to entertain, educate and inspire you. We aim to distribute these through every available channel with every available technology—whether that means you are seeing anarchist classics at our bookfair stalls; reading our latest vegan cookbook at the café; downloading geeky fiction e-books; or digging new music and timely videos from our website.

PM Press is always on the lookout for talented and skilled volunteers, artists, activists and writers to work with. If you have a great idea for a project or can contribute in some way, please get in touch.

PM Press
PO Box 23912
Oakland CA 94623
510-658-3906
www.pmpress.org

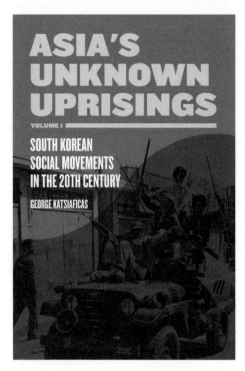

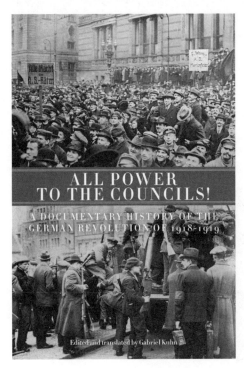

ALSO AVAILABLE FROM PM PRESS

The Red Army Faction, A Documentary History - Volume 1: Projectiles For the People

Edited by J. Smith
and André Moncourt

978-1-60486-029-0
$34.95

The first in a two-volume series, this is by far the most in-depth political history of the Red Army Faction ever made available in English.

Projectiles for the People starts its story in the days following World War II, showing how American imperialism worked hand in glove with the old pro-Nazi ruling class, shaping West Germany into an authoritarian anti-communist bulwark and launching pad for its aggression against Third World nations. The volume also recounts the opposition that emerged from intellectuals, communists, independent leftists, and then—explosively—the radical student movement and countercultural revolt of the 1960s.

It was from this revolt that the Red Army Faction emerged, an underground organization devoted to carrying out armed attacks within the Federal Republic of Germany, in the view of establishing a tradition of illegal, guerilla resistance to imperialism and state repression. Through its bombs and manifestos the RAF confronted the state with opposition at a level many activists today might find difficult to imagine.

For the first time ever in English, this volume presents all of the manifestos and communiqués issued by the RAF between 1970 and 1977, from Andreas Baader's prison break, through the 1972 May Offensive and the 1975 hostage-taking in Stockholm, to the desperate, and tragic, events of the "German Autumn" of 1977.

Drawing on both mainstream and movement sources, this book is intended as a contribution to the comrades of today—and to the comrades of tomorrow—both as testimony to those who struggled before and as an explanation as to how they saw the world, why they made the choices they made, and the price they were made to pay for having done so.

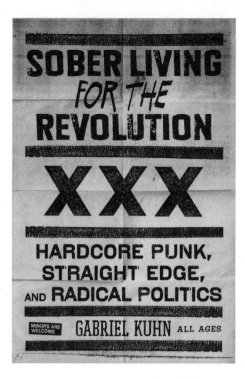

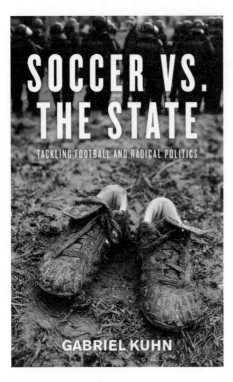

Soccer has turned into a multi-billion dollar industry. Professionalism and commercialization dominate its global image. Yet the game retains a rebellious side, maybe more so than any other sport co-opted by money makers and corrupt politicians. From its roots in working-class England to political protests by players and fans, and a current radical soccer underground, the notion of football as the "people's game" has been kept alive by numerous individuals, teams, and communities.

This book not only traces this history, but also reflects on common criticisms: soccer ferments nationalism, serves right-wing powers, fosters competitiveness. Acknowledging these concerns, alternative perspectives on the game are explored, down to practical examples of egalitarian DIY soccer!

Soccer vs. the State serves both as an orientation for the politically conscious football supporter and as an inspiration for those who try to pursue the love of the game away from television sets and big stadiums, bringing it to back alleys and muddy pastures.

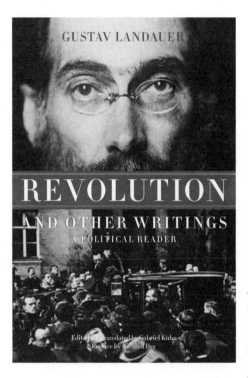

ALSO AVAILABLE FROM PM PRESS

Revolution and Other Writings:
A Political Reader

Gustav Landauer
Edited and Translated by
Gabriel Kuhn

978-1-60486-054-2
$26.95

"Landauer is the most important agitator of the radical and revolutionary movement in the entire country." This is how Gustav Landauer is described in a German police file from 1893. Twenty-six years later, Landauer would die at the hands of reactionary soldiers who overthrew the Bavarian Council Republic, a three-week attempt to realize libertarian socialism amidst the turmoil of post-World War I Germany. It was the last chapter in the life of an activist, writer, and mystic who Paul Avrich calls "the most influential German anarchist intellectual of the twentieth century."

This is the first comprehensive collection of Landauer writings in English. It includes one of his major works, *Revolution*, thirty additional essays and articles, and a selection of correspondence. The texts cover Landauer's entire political biography, from his early anarchism of the 1890s to his philosophical reflections at the turn of the century, the subsequent establishment of the Socialist Bund, his tireless agitation against the war, and the final days among the revolutionaries in Munich. Additional chapters collect Landauer's articles on radical politics in the US and Mexico, and illustrate the scope of his writing with texts on corporate capital, language, education, and Judaism. The book includes an extensive introduction, commentary, and bibliographical information, compiled by the editor and translator Gabriel Kuhn as well as a preface by Richard Day.

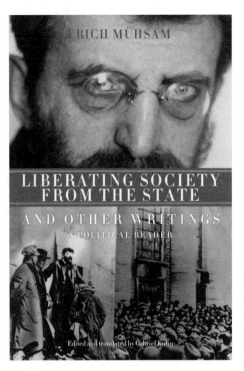

ALSO AVAILABLE FROM PM PRESS

Liberating Society from the State and Other Writings: A Political Reader

Erich Mühsam
Edited by Gabriel Kuhn

978-1-60486-055-9
$26.95

Erich Mühsam (1878-1934), poet, bohemian, revolutionary, is one of Germany's most renowned and influential anarchists. Born into a middle-class Jewish family, he challenged the conventions of bourgeois society at the turn of the century, engaged in heated debates on the rights of women and homosexuals, and traveled Europe in search of radical communes and artist colonies. He was a primary instigator of the ill-fated Bavarian Council Republic in 1919, and held the libertarian banner high during a Weimar Republic that came under increasing threat by right-wing forces. In 1933, four weeks after Hitler's ascension to power, Mühsam was arrested in his Berlin home. He spent the last sixteen months of his life in detention and died in the Oranienburg Concentration Camp in July 1934.

Mühsam wrote poetry, plays, essays, articles, and diaries. His work unites a burning desire for individual liberation with anarcho-communist convictions, and bohemian strains with syndicalist tendencies. The body of his writings is immense, yet hardly any English translations exist. This collection presents not only *Liberating Society from the State: What is Communist Anarchism?*, Mühsam's main political pamphlet and one of the key texts in the history of German anarchism, but also some of his best-known poems, unbending defenses of political prisoners, passionate calls for solidarity with the lumpenproletariat, recollections of the utopian community of Monte Verità, debates on the rights of homosexuals and women, excerpts from his journals, and essays contemplating German politics and anarchist theory as much as Jewish identity and the role of intellectuals in the class struggle.

An appendix documents the fate of Zenzl Mühsam, who, after her husband's death, escaped to the Soviet Union where she spent twenty years in Gulag camps.

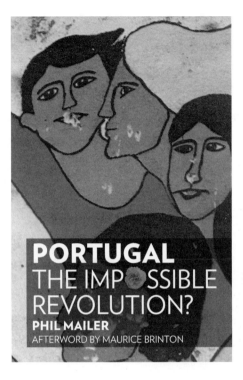

The CNT in the Spanish Revolution is the history of one of the most original and audacious, and arguably also the most far-reaching, of all the twentieth-century revolutions. It is the history of the giddy years of political change and hope in 1930s Spain, when the so-called 'Generation of '36', Peirats' own generation, rose up against the oppressive structures of Spanish society. It is also a history of a revolution that failed, crushed in the jaws of its enemies on both the reformist left and the reactionary right.

José Peirats' account is effectively the official CNT history of the war, passionate, partisan but, above all, intelligent. Its huge sweeping canvas covers all areas of the anarchist experience—the spontaneous militias, the revolutionary collectives, the moral dilemmas occasioned by the clash of revolutionary ideals and the stark reality of the war effort against Franco and his German Nazi and Italian Fascist allies.

This new edition is carefully indexed in a way that converts the work into a usable tool for historians and makes it much easier for the general reader to dip in with greater purpose and pleasure.

Moments of Excess: Movements, Protest and Everyday Life

The Free Association

978-1-60486-113-6
$14.95

The first decade of the twenty-first century was marked by a series of global summits which seemed to assume ever-greater importance —from the WTO ministerial meeting in Seattle at the end of 1999, through the G8 summits at Genoa, Evian and Gleneagles, up to the United Nations Climate Change Conference (COP15) at Copenhagen in 2009.

But these global summits did not pass uncontested. Alongside and against them, there unfolded a different version of globalization. *Moments of Excess* is a collection of texts which offer an insider analysis of this cycle of counter-summit mobilisations. It weaves lucid descriptions of the intensity of collective action into a more sober reflection on the developing problematics of the 'movement of movements'. The collection examines essential questions concerning the character of anti-capitalist movements, and the very meaning of movement; the relationship between intensive collective experiences—'moments of excess'—and 'everyday life'; and the tensions between open, all-inclusive, 'constitutive' practices, on the one hand, and the necessity of closure, limits and antagonism, on the other.

Moments of Excess includes a new introduction explaining the origin of the texts and their relation to event-based politics, and a postscript which explores new possibilities for anti-capitalist movements in the midst of crisis.

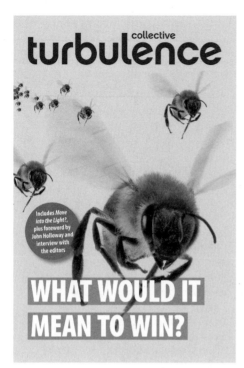